THE DEVELOPMENT
OF THE
TELEVISION NETWORK OLIGOPOLY

This is a volume in the
Arno Press collection

DISSERTATIONS IN BROADCASTING

Advisory Editor
Christopher H. Sterling

*See last pages of this volume
for a complete list of titles.*

THE DEVELOPMENT
OF THE
TELEVISION NETWORK OLIGOPOLY

Stewart Louis Long

ARNO PRESS
A New York Times Company
New York • 1979

Editorial Supervision: Andrea Hicks

————◆————

First publication 1979 by Arno Press Inc.
Copyright © 1979 by Stewart Louis Long

DISSERTATIONS IN BROADCASTING
ISBN for complete set: 0-405-11754-X
See last pages of this volume for titles.

Manufactured in the United States of America

————◆————

Library of Congress Cataloging in Publication Data

Long, Stewart Louis.
    The development of the television network oligopoly.

    (Dissertations in broadcasting)
    Originally presented as the author's thesis, Univer-
sity of Illinois at Urbana-Champaign, 1974.
    Bibliography: p.
    1. Television broadcasting--United States.
2. Oligopolies--United States. I. Title. II. Series.
HE8700.8.L65 1979   384.55'43   78-21725
ISBN 0-405-11764-7

THE DEVELOPMENT OF THE TELEVISION NETWORK OLIGOPOLY

BY

STEWART LOUIS LONG

B.A., City University (New York), 1970
A.M., University of Illinois, 1972

THESIS

Submitted in partial fulfillment of the requirements
for the degree of Doctor of Philosophy in Economics
in the Graduate College of the
University of Illinois at Urbana-Champaign, 1974

Urbana, Illinois

THE DEVELOPMENT OF THE TELEVISION NETWORK OLIGOPOLY

Stewart Louis Long, Ph.D.
Department of Economics
University of Illinois at Urbana-Champaign, 1974

This study traces historically the development of the network
oligopoly in the commercial television broadcasting industry, and
examines some of the concomitant effects on the ultimate consumer of
the industry's product, the television viewing public. Since the first
network television broadcasts take place in 1946, the main narrative in
this work starts with that year. It ends with the year 1956, rather
than the present, because the industry's structure had attained its
present stage by the mid-1950's and has remained relatively unchanged
since then.

The study has two, equally important, points of emphasis. The
first is the attempt to answer the questions of how and why, after only
ten years of operations, concentration in television broadcasting had
reached the level where three firms accounted for almost 50 percent of
industry revenues and 45 percent of industry profits. The second point
pursued is the question of the relationship between industry concentration and industry performance.

For the purposes of this study, performance consists of both a
"private" and a "public" component. The private component is measured
by profitability. The public component is measured by the expenditure
upon, and the diversity of, television programming. Such a scheme for
evaluating performance was purposely chosen in order to determine
whether, historically, there have been economic forces operating in the
industry which have led to an improving private performance for the

broadcasters of television programming and a simultaneously deteriorating public performance for the viewers of this programming.

The study finds that a combination of advertiser-support and government regulation, television's legacy from radio which preceeded it, led to the existence of a strong network triopoly in 1956. Private performance in this highly concentrated industry was excellent, particularly in comparison to earlier years, before the networks had consolidated their power. At the same time, it is also found that while network program expenditures may have positively affected programming quality, network program schedules negatively affected programming diversity. This evidence leads credence to the hypothesis that there was indeed a divergence between private and public performance in television broadcasting as the network oligopoly developed.

The study concludes by noting that the factors which are responsible for this divergence between private and public performance still operate today in the television industry. Since these factors are part of the foundations of American commercial broadcasting, there seems little hope that the situation is in any way self-correcting, and the only way the welfare of the viewing public is to be significantly improved may be through the medium of "public television."

ACKNOWLEDGEMENT

The author wishes to acknowledge with gratitude the guidance and consideration of Donald L. Kemmerer, the chairman of his dissertation committee, and of the remaining members of the committee: Larry D. Neal, Thomas S. Friedland, and Joseph D. Phillips. Also a special note of thanks goes to Allan I. Duchan for his invaluable aid in preparing a computer program for calculating the values of the television program diversity indices which appear in this study.

TABLE OF CONTENTS

LIST OF TABLES

LIST OF FIGURES

CHAPTER I

INTRODUCTION

...the fusion of economic strength and information control,
or image-making, ...or call it what you will, is the new
quintessence of power...
                              -- Herbert I. Schiller
          Mass Communications and American Empire. p. 1.

Networks ...have a virtual monopoly of a whole media of
communications. ...[they] represent a concentration of
power over [the] American public ...unknown in history.
                              -- Spiro T. Agnew
          The New York Times. November 14, 1961. p. 24.

As the above quotes are meant to imply, criticism of network

power in television broadcasting has come from a wide variety of

sources, ranging from Schiller on the left to Agnew on the right in

the political spectrum. Although there undoubtedly would be much

disagreement among these critics concerning exactly what the effects

of this power are, there probably would be little disagreement among

them that the industry's oligopoly market structure is the source of

the networks' power.

The purpose of this study is to trace historically the develop-

ment of the network oligopoly in the television broadcasting

industry[1], and to examine some of the concomitant effects on the

ultimate consumer of the industry's product, the television viewing

public. Since the first network television broadcasting begins in

1946, the main narrative in this work starts with that year. It

terminates with the year 1956, rather than the present, because

the industry's structure had attained its present stage by 1956,

and has remained relatively unchanged since then. The main

evidence to support this is that no network has entered nor left the industry since DuMont ceased its national operations in 1955. In addition, network concentration ratios have remained relatively constant in almost every facet of the industry since 1956.

Scope and Method of the Study

This study has two, equally important, points of emphasis. The first is an attempt to answer the questions of how and why, after only ten years of operations, three networks accounted for almost fifty percent of all revenues and forty-five percent of all profits in the television broadcasting industry. The second point pursued is the question of the relationship, if any, between industry concentration and industry performance in television broadcasting.

For the purposes of this study, performance consists of both a "private" and a "public" component. The private component is measured by profitability. The public component is measured by the expenditure upon, and the diversity of, television programming. Such a scheme for evaluating performance has been purposely chosen in order to examine whether, historically, there have been economic forces operating in the industry which have led to an improving private performance for the broadcasters of television programming and a simultaneously deteriorating public performance for the viewers of this programming.

The study consists of six chapters. The remainder of this first chapter develops some relatively simple economic theory which

would lead one to expect both the development of networks and therefore concentration in commercial broadcasting, and a divergence
between public and private performance in the industry.

The second chapter presents background material concerning radio
broadcasting which is essential to the understanding of subsequent
developments in television broadcasting. The major emphasis is on
explaining how the advertiser-support nature of broadcasting arose
in radio, how this in turn led to the formation of national radio
networks, and how government regulation developed in broadcasting.

The third chapter looks at the early years of television, with
emphasis on the period 1946 to 1948 when television networking
begins. The experimental nature and unprofitability of broadcasting
both at the station, and network, level is examined. This chapter
also deals with the Federal Communications Commission's decision in
1948 to "freeze" the allocation of television station licenses until
it could work out a coherent "master plan" for the new medium.

The fourth chapter concerns the development of the television
networks during the "freeze" years, 1949 to 1952. It shows that the
length and nature of the "freeze" had substantially different effects
on the A.B.C. and DuMont networks than on the N.B.C. and C.B.S. networks. It points out that as this period drew to a close, N.B.C.
and C.B.S. dominated the television industry just as they had earlier
dominated the radio industry.

The fifth chapter examines the development of the network oligopoly into its final form during the "post-freeze" period, 1953-
1956. The problems which arose from the "uneconomic" station

allocation plan which the F.C.C. had adopted in ending the "freeze" late in 1952 are looked at. Also pointed out is the growing aware- ness and criticism of the networks' power in the industry during this period. Finally, the decision by the F.C.C. to allow a merger between A.B.C. and United Paramount Theatres, Inc., is examined for the effects it had on A.B.C., DuMont, and the industry as a whole.

The sixth and final chapter presents a summary of the develop- ment of the industry's structure into a powerful triopoly, and conclusions concerning the relationship of this development to the industry's performance, both private and public.

The Economics of Commercial Television Broadcasting

The advertiser-support nature of commercial television broad- casting acts as a constraint which determines how the market for programming operates. An hour (or some other convenient, pre- determined time period) of programming is purchased (sponsored) as a vehicle for an advertiser to air his commercial message on. The direct participants in the market for programming are the stations or networks who are the sellers, and advertisers who are the buyers. Thus the ultimate consumer of the programs broadcast -- the viewing public, does not participate in the market where the prices of programming are determined. As a result, viewer satisfaction (i.e. "utility"), or dissatisfaction (i.e. "disutility"), is in fact external to the operation of the market for programming. The wel- fare of viewers may therefore be unaffected, or positively or per- versely affected by the efficient operation of the market for pro- gramming.

That the operation of the market for programming will lead to
the link-up of stations into networks is illustrated in Figure I-1.
Depicted is the operation of the market in determining the price for
one hour of any station's prime time[2] (6-11 p.m.) programming.
First, looking at the supply side of the situation, a station's
supply curve for programming, S_1, is almost perfectly price elastic,
since increases in marginal cost due to increased hours of programming are negligible, until a full schedule (5 hours) of prime time
programming is being offered. After this point, the supply curve
becomes completely price inelastic, since it is physically impossible
to offer additional hours of programming during prime time.

Looking now at the demand side of the picture, D_1 represents the
demand curve of advertisers for prime time programming on a station
such as the one under consideration with a given potential audience
size (circulation). Such a station, being an oligopolistic competitor in most, and without competitors in the remaining, markets,
realizes the downward sloping nature of the demand curve it faces.
Nevertheless, the demand for television programming is price elastic,
since there are relatively good substitutes for it such as newspaper
and magazine space. Therefore, assuming the marginal revenue curve
MR_1 which stems from the demand D_1 intersects the station's supply
curve S_1 at point F, where it is completely price inelastic, the
result is that the station will offer for sale a full schedule of
prime time programming, quantity Q^*. It will be able to set a price
for each hour of this programming of P_1, and therefore realize a
profit represented by rectangle $ABGP_1$.

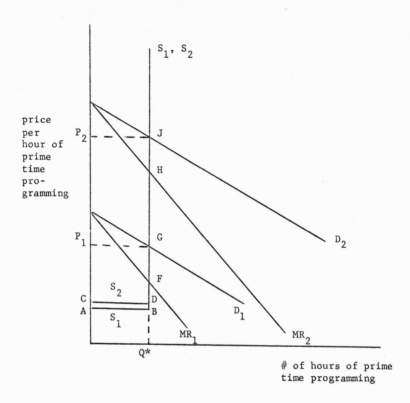

Figure I-1:   The Market for a Television Stations's
              Prime Time Programming

Note: Q* - a full schedule (5 hours)

Now it will be assumed that there is another station in a different city with the same cost structure and circulation as the station depicted in Figure I-1. If these two stations are operated independently, each would realize a profit represented by rectangle $ABGP_1$. But if instead they link-up and broadcast the same programs simultaneously, the result is that their combined supply schedule, S_2, will be slightly above S_1 in its price elastic section, due to the interconnection cost. But in its price inelastic section, S_2 is identical to S_1 since the linked-up stations still have only five hours of programming to sell to advertisers. However, since advertisers are now buying time on a link-up with double the circulation that either station had by itself, D_2 is now the relevant demand curve of advertisers for programming broadcast to twice the potential audience, and MR_2 is the relevant marginal revenue curve. The result is that the intersection of MR_2 and S_2 cause the link-up to also offer a full schedule of prime time programming, quantity Q^*. Only now the price which this primitive network sets for each hour of this programming is P_2. The profit earning by the linked-up stations together is represented by rectangle $CDJP_2$, which is larger than the doubled area of rectangle $ABGP_1$ which the two stations would have earned if operated independently of one another. Furthermore, each time an additional station is added to the link-up, the relevant demand curve of advertisers is again shifted outward, but with a less than proportionate increase in costs. Thus the advertiser-support nature of commercial broadcasting which ties advertisers' demand for programming to circulation, combined with the economies of scale in programming which station link-ups provide, make the tendency for stations to link up into networks seem almost inevitable.

Once the trend toward networking has begun, the regulatory process has a tendency to maintain and reinforce the economic power of the already existing firms and to act as a barrier to entry, particularly at the network scale of operation. It does so because the Federal Communications Commission has traditionally had two major goals with respect to the providing of television broadcasting service to the public. These goals are the non-termination of service (i.e. survival of the firm), and the improvement of service (i.e. programming innovation). Based upon these two goals, and assuming it gives each equal weight, the F.C.C. can be expected to utilize the following decision rules in deciding whether to allocate a television station to an existing network or to a new entrant.

Let: S_e = the probability of survival of an existing network.

S_n = the probability of survival of a new entrant.

I_e = the probability of programming innovation by an existing network.

I_n = the probability of programming innovation by a new entrant.

Then if:

$$S_e + I_e > S_n + I_n \qquad (I.1)$$

The existing network will be awarded the station allocation.

But if:

$$S_n + I_n > S_e + I_e \qquad (I.2)$$

The new entrant will be awarded the station allocation.

Given the propensity of new businesses in general to fail more

often than established firms, combined with the limited number of
stations available for link-ups into national networks, it can be
assumed that in general:

$$S_e > S_n \qquad (I.3)$$

Concerning the probability of programming innovation, the
picture is less clear. Some would make a Schumpeterian argument
that the resources coming from the profits of the established
oligopoly firms are needed if programming innovation is to take
place, and therefore, the existing networks are the more likely
innovators. Others would argue that a new entrant, in attempting to
"break into" an oligopoly market, would be more likely to program
innovate in an attempt to "differentiate" its product from those of
its established competitors. Still others might claim that neither
existing networks nor new entrants are likely to display any con-
sistent pattern of being either more or less likely to program
innovate. Thus any one of the following assumptions could be made:

$$I_e > I_n \qquad (I.4)$$

$$I_e = I_n \qquad (I.5)$$

$$I_n > I_e \qquad (I.6)$$

If either equation (I.4) or equation (I.5) is the correct
assumption concerning the probability of program innovation, then
by adding either of them to equation (I.3), the result is:

$$S_e + I_e > S_n + I_n \qquad (I.1)$$

and therefore the existing network will be awarded the station
allocation.

This leaves only to consider the results should equation (I.6) be the correct assumption concerning the probability of program innovation. If indeed it is correct, the question is whether the new entrant's superior innovation outweighs the existing network's survival abilities. The fact that there is a disagreement concerning the newcomer's innovative edge, leads to the conclusion that the new entrant's comparative advantage in innovation probability is less than the existing network's similar advantage in survival probability. We can express this in the following manner:

$$S_e - S_n > I_n - I_e \qquad (I.7)$$

If we now add to equation (I.7) the following identity:

$$S_n + I_e = S_n + I_e \qquad (I.8)$$

the result is:

$$S_e + I_e > S_n + I_n \qquad (I.1)$$

and therefore in this, as in the previous cases, the existing network will be awarded the station allocation.

Often the argument is made that regulatory agencies make decisions favoring the vested interests in the industries which they oversee for political reasons. But it has been shown that the F.C.C. in rationally implementing its primary goals with respect to providing television service, political considerations aside, would most likely always allocate stations to existing networks, thus reinforcing existing network power, and acting as a barrier to entry for new networks.

Having seen that commercial television stations would normally tend to link up in networks, and that regulation tends to maintain this horizontal concentration, it can also be illustrated why such an industry might have a divergence between its private and public performance. That private performance will tend to improve in such an industry seems likely, since almost any oligopoly theory would lead us to expect more than "normal" profits to be generated. But what is just as likely to occur is that diversity of programming in an oligopolized broadcasting industry will suffer.[3]

Studies have shown that television viewers have preferences among program types.[4] These program types can be separated into two categories: 1. "mass appeal" programs, or those preferred with a high degree of substitutibility among types by the major portion (70-80%) of television viewers, 2. "specialized appeal" programs, or those preferred with a low degree of substitutibility among types by the remaining minority (20-30%) of television viewers.[5]

Referring back to Figure I-1, it was noted that the price of an hour of programming is determined by the position of the demand curve of advertisers, which in turn is determined by the size of the potential audience to which the programming is broadcast. But whether any particular hour of programming is actually sold, depends upon the proportion of that potential audience which advertisers believe will be watching that particular hour of programming. As a result, any station or network will, in order to sell all of its prime time programming hours, attempt to maximize its actual share of the total audience watching at every hour. In deciding whether to ever broadcast "specialized appeal" programs which only a minority of viewers

might watch, a station or network would utilize the following
decision rule:

>Let: k = that percentage of the total audience with "mass
>appeal" program preferences.
>
>j = the largest percentage of the total audience with
>some common "specialized appeal" program
>preference.
>
>x = the number of stations or networks in the market.

Then if:

$$j > \frac{k}{x} \tag{I.9}$$

a station or network might broadcast "specialized appeal" programs.

But if:

$$\frac{k}{x} > j \tag{I.10}$$

a station or network would be reluctant to broadcast "specialized
appeal" programs.

An example of how this might work is as follows:

Assume: k = 80 percent.

>j = 15 percent (which is optimistic, given the
>fragmentation of the "specialized appeal"
>audience).
>
>x = 3 stations or networks.

In this case, the value of $\frac{k}{x}$, 26.6 percent, is greater than the
value of j, 15 percent. Therefore each station or network can
capture a greater share of the total audience by presenting "mass
appeal" programming and sharing this 80 percent of the total audience
with its competitors. To present "specialized appeal" programming,
while commendable from an altruistic viewpoint, would be irrational
given the advertiser-support nature of commercial broadcasting. At

best this would capture only 15 percent of the total audience, and at

the same time possibly allow the two competing stations or networks

to capture up to 40 percent of the total audience each, by continuing

to broadcast "mass appeal" programming. Since the numbers in this

example are fairly good approximations of the actual situation as it

exists in the television industry, it is understandable that each

member of a network oligopoly would tend to broadcast ever-increasing

amounts of "mass appeal" programming.

Perhaps one of the clearest statements of the connection between

the lack of program diversity which may result from this, and the

welfare of television viewers, and one which will serve as the

rationale for including diversity as a major component of the public

performance in the television industry which this study seeks to

examine, was made in a report issued by the President's Task Force

on Communications Policy in June of 1969. That report stated:

> The television industry does not provide a full range
> of programming choices. ...Little programming is directed
> toward the needs, tastes or interests of ethnic, cultural
> or economic minorities.
> As a result, two groups of citizens suffer. In the
> first place, a substantial minority of Americans rarely
> watch television at all. For them, television offers
> nothing comparable to material available in print and at
> theatres, to which they accordingly turn to satisfy their
> leisure time information and entertainment desires.
> In the second place, and possibly more important,
> many individuals who are presently frequent television
> watchers derive less satisfaction from the current
> program fare than they would if a wider diversity of
> choices were available. When programming sources are
> limited, as they are now, the programmer aims at a very
> large audience; hence, his programming reflects a
> common denominator of interests and tastes. His programs
> are apt to satisfy the third or fourth preferences of many.
> But they will satisfy the first preferences of fewer. More
> variety would, in other words, serve not only those members

of the population who are now left out of the television
audience altogether; it would also increase the satisfaction of present viewers who would on occasion prefer
specialized offerings more than the programs guaranteed
to attract a mass audience.[6]

It has now been shown that economic theory would lead one to

expect that: 1. station link-ups, i.e. networks, would develop in

television broadcasting, 2. regulation would maintain and reinforce

existing networks' power, acting as a barrier to entry for new net-

works, 3. oligopoly in television broadcasting, while boding well

for profitability, would bode ill for program diversity. To a large

extent this theory results from the operation of two institutional

factors, the advertiser-support nature of commercial broadcasting,

and government regulation. In the next chapter, how both these

factors developed in the radio broadcasting industry, and thus became

part of that industry's legacy to television, will be shown.

FOOTNOTES FOR CHAPTER I

[1]This study is concerned only with commercial television broadcasting, and will not deal with the "public" or "educational" segments of television broadcasting, neither of which was large during the period under consideration.

[2]Prices of programming in other than the prime time period are usually calculated as a fraction of the prime time price.

[3]Much of the following discussion of the relationship between oligopoly and diversity in broadcasting is based upon an article by Peter O. Steiner, "Program Patterns and Preferences and the Workability of Competition in Radio Broadcasting," Quarterly Journal of Economics, LXVI, (May, 1952), pp. 194-223.

[4]Gary Steiner, The People Look at Television: A Study of Audience Attitudes, (New York: Alfred A. Knopf, 1963), esp. pp. 115-160.

[5]The classification of various program types into "mass appeal" or "specialized appeal" categories is presented for this study in Appendix A, Table 1, p. 136.

[6]U.S. President's Task Force on Communications Policy, Staff Paper Six - Part I, (Washington, D.C., 1969), pp. 51-52.

CHAPTER II

THE RISE OF NETWORKS -- THE RADIO EXPERIENCE

The course which the development of the television network
oligopoly took was determined to a large extent by events that had
occurred many years earlier in the radio broadcasting industry. In
tracing the story of commercial broadcasting in radio it will be
shown that networks became an integral part of that industry, and as
such provided the example for, as well as fostering most of the
companies involved in, the operation of networks in television
broadcasting.

Radio as we know it today was the culmination of many years of
gradual invention, innovation, and entrepreneurship, which began in
the late nineteenth century. But it was not until the 1920's that
it was fully realized that radio was fundamentally different from
the earlier electronic communications media, the telephone and the
telegraph. In the search for a method to exploit profitably this new
medium, advertising eventually was struck upon as a source of income
for broadcasting. With this source of financial support established,
the rise of national radio networks became almost inevitable.

The Scientific Origins of Radio

As is the case with many other modern scientific developments,
it can be said that no one man was the inventor of the radio. As
early as 1864, the British physicist James C. Maxwell was able to
predict the properties of electromagnetic waves in theory, long

before their actual existence was suspected. In 1887 a German
scientist, Heinrich Hertz, through the use of electrical oscilla-
tions, created electromagnetic waves such as those whose existence
Maxwell had predicted. These were soon dubbed "Hertzian waves" and
would be the foundation upon which modern radio is based, despite
the fact that Hertz himself doubted that the waves would ever have
any practical value.[1]

But it took the imagination of an Italian who was not a trained
scientist, Guglielmo Marconi, to demonstrate that "Hertzian waves"
had an eminently practical application, telegraphing without wires.
Marconi secured a patent for wireless telegraphy in Britain in 1897,
a mere three years after his first introduction to the theory of
"Hertzian waves" in a magazine article he read while vacationing in
the Alps.[2] His experiments and demonstrations were attended with
so much publicity that the simultaneous explorations into the
possibilities of wireless telegraphy by Oliver Lodge in Britain,
Alexander Popov in Russia, Adolphus Slaby in Germany, and Edouard
Branly in France, were pushed into the background, and Marconi
became, in the minds of most Americans at least, the inventor of
the "wireless."

But Marconi's contribution was really a development in telegraphy, and there remained a final hurdle to be overcome before
radio as we know it was born. This final obstacle was the problem
of how to transmit the human voice without wires, and it was solved
by the invention of the vacuum tube in 1904 by a British engineer,
John A. Fleming, and its further refinement by a Canadian,

Reginald Fessenden, and an American, Lee DeForest. Although the latter two became embroiled in patent litigation and personal animosities that "make it difficult to draw an accurate picture of the sequence of scientific events,"[3] it seems generally agreed upon that Fessenden's Christmas Eve broadcast of 1906 was actually the first to transmit voices.[4] Radio was born, but the broadcasting industry was still a long way off.

The New Medium

Although Fessenden, DeForest, and others, used the broadcasting of music, news and other information in an attempt to publicize the development of the "wireless", they and other early radio entrepreneurs at first considered radio to be a new type of point-to-point communication which might be substituted for the existing telegraph and telephone. Thus radio in its early years was most often referred to as either wireless telegraphy or radio telephony.

A number of companies ventured into the development of the new medium in America. The first, set up in 1899, was American Marconi, a subsidiary of British Marconi, the firm which held all of Marconi's patents, and the leading "wireless" manufacturer in the world. This company "soon came to control almost all of our commercial wireless communications, then limited to ship to shore transmissions and special point-to-point broadcasts."[5]

Before long, however, a number of native American companies started doing research in radio, and after a number of new patents were won, such as that for the Alexanderson alternator, they entered the equipment manufacturing business in competition with the

dominant American Marconi. These new entrants included General

Electric (G.E.), Westinghouse, and Western Electric, a subsidiary of

the American Telephone and Telegraph Company (A.T.&T.).[6] In addition

to these companies, much experimentation and even manufacturing was

being carried on by individuals on a small scale, with little or no

hope of ever turning a profit. All this activity resulted in a spate

of conflicting patent claims and endless litigation which brought

the manufacturing of radio apparatus in the United States almost to a

halt by the eve of World War I. It took the war to rationalize the

confused and chaotic American radio industry.

As Sydney Head points out in Broadcasting in America:

> World War I caused a great acceleration in the ...
> development of wireless communication.
> ...The United States Navy took over the operation
> of all private stations that it could usefully employ,
> and required the shutting down and disassembling of all
> other transmitters. In order to capitalize fully on all
> United States patents, the Navy effected a kind of
> moratorium on patent suits. This resulted in a pooling
> of the country's total technical resources which
> previously had been quite impossible because of commercial
> rivalries.
> In short, wireless advanced tremendously during the
> war, and came back to civilian life with materially altered
> status. The pre-war era had been dominated by the inventor-[7]
> entrepreneurs. Now began the era of big business.

After the war, transmitting stations were returned to their

owners, and patent rights reverted to their private holders. It

soon became apparent that if nothing were done, the pre-war conflict

and confusion might re-appear in the industry. As a result, a first

step in the possible solution of the industry's problems was taken

by General Electric in 1919, when, under the direction of Rear

Admiral W. H. G. Bullard, the Navy's Director of Communications, it
formed a new company, The Radio Corporation of America (R.C.A.).
R.C.A. bought all the patents and assets of American Marconi, thus
forestalling what was feared by some, especially the Navy, might
become a foreign monopoly of the American radio industry.[8] It is
interesting to note that at this point in time, equipment manufacture
was considered to be the only important part of the radio business,
and broadcasting was not yet a tangible factor in corporate decisions
in the industry. As Owen D. Young, the G.E. vice-president in charge
of the R.C.A. venture, later testified: "We had no broadcasting in
our minds in 1919 and 1920."[9]

Westinghouse and A.T.&T. also became stockholders in the newly
formed R.C.A., and so the second step in solving the radio industry's
problems could now be put into action. R.C.A., as a jointly owned
subsidiary of the major patent holders in the radio field, was to be
the vehicle that would avoid a post-war industry stalemate. Starting
in 1920, a series of cross-licensing agreements were reached between
R.C.A., Westinghouse, and G.E., known as the "radio group", and
A.T.&T. and its subsidiary Western Electric, known as the "telephone
group".[10] These agreements pooled all patents related to radio, and
in effect "divided the field", allowing G.E. and Westinghouse the
exclusive right to manufacture wireless receiving equipment, R.C.A.
the exclusive right to sell such receivers, and reserving to A.T.&T.
and Western Electric the exclusive right to manufacture, lease, or
sell, wireless transmitting equipment.[11]

At last it was thought, peace was at hand in the radio industry.
But later events would shatter what was in effect but a temporary
cease-fire.

The Dawn of Commercial Broadcasting

Up until the 1920's, critics maintained that the greatest
weakness of radio communication as a commercial enterprise, was its
lack of secrecy. One could not limit the reception of one's broadcasts to authorized listeners only. This may seem a strange attitude
to someone familiar with the modern operations of radio broadcasting,
but as Head points out:

> The whole history and tradition, first of wire and
> then of wireless communication, had emphasized that
> commercial profit was to be derived from the exchange of
> private intelligence ... The sender paid a fee for the
> use of the service, just as today one pays by the word
> to send a telegram or by the call to use a telephone.
> How else could a profit be made? What possible motive
> could a sender have for paying money to reach an unknown
> audience indiscriminately?[12]

Probably no single person is responsible for the final realiza-
tion that radio's lack of secrecy was in fact a possible strength
rather than a weakness, but Lee DeForest and David Sarnoff were
among the earliest to articulate the idea of radio's potential as a
public rather than a private medium. As early as 1909 DeForest is
reported to have said, "I look forward to the day when by means of
radio, opera may be brought into every home. Some day the news,
even advertising will be sent out to the public on the wireless
telephone."[13] And in 1916, Sarnoff, then an engineer with American
Marconi, wrote a letter to the general manager of that company

stating that he had in mind a "plan of development" to make radio a "household utility", and that he envisioned the use of the radio to transmit recorded music, live concerts, lectures, and even up-to-the-minute baseball scores to the public.[14]

But these two were visionaries, and it wasn't until November of 1920, that the first commercial broadcasting station, KDKA in Pittsburgh, went on the air, broadcasting the returns of the Cox-Harding Presidential election as its first program.[15]

But if big business had been slow to realize the potential of radio broadcasting, the public was not. "The new idea of radio as a public broadcast medium caught the imagination of the American people and spread like wildfire."[16] Sales of radio receivers climbed from $2 million in 1920 to $136 million in 1923.[17] And this does not even take into account the many people who did not buy finished sets, but rather built their own, or had a knowledgeable friend build it, from parts, the sales of which to the public totaled $75 million in 1923.[18]

Most broadcasting stations were set up and operated by companies which manufactured and sold radio receiving equipment. These companies saw broadcasting as a necessary expense in order to stimulate and maintain the demand for their primary product, apparatus. And in these primitive days of broadcasting, very little was required in the way of operating expenditure once the transmitting equipment had been purchased. Programming costs were virtually nil, since "the main desire of many listeners was to be able to pick up on their battery-operated crystal headphone receivers the call

letters of distant stations. Programs at first were really excuses
for many stations to go on the air so that they might fulfill their
true mission of announcing their call letters."[19] Both performers
and technical personnel of most stations offered their services at
little or no cost in order to be part of the exciting new world of
radio broadcasting.

After a while, however, the novelty began to wear off. Performers and other station personnel demanded payment for their
services, and the profit margin on equipment sales began to be
squeezed by the increasing costs to manufacturers of operating
broadcasting stations which of themselves earned nothing. As
Erik Barnouw notes:

> The question, "how will broadcasting be financed?"
> had hardly been asked in 1921. During 1922 it became a
> conversational topic. In 1923 and 1924 it was asked
> with increasing urgency. In 1925 it reached a crisis
> stage.[20]

It is interesting to note that in early discussions of this
question, the eventual answer, advertising support, was not considered to be the best, nor even the most likely, solution to the
problem. There were two reasons for this. First, it was considered
debasing to the medium and in bad taste to use radio to advertise
goods for sale. Thus we have then Secretary of Commerce, Herbert
Hoover saying in 1922, "It is inconceivable that we should allow
so great a possibility for service, for news, for entertainment, for
education, and for vital commercial purposes to be drowned in advertising chatter."[21] Second, it was doubted by some that radio could
ever compete successfully as an advertising medium with newspapers
and magazines.

The plan for financing broadcasting which was most often proposed, and which seemed most likely eventually to be adopted, was one where a tax or fee would be assessed on all receiving sets and parts manufactured in the country. In effect there would have been a sales tax on radio equipment to be borne by the manufacturers and the consumers of radio apparatus in varying degrees depending on the method of collection and the price elasticity of demand for radios. Although seriously discussed for many years, the actual mechanics of such a plan could never be satisfactory worked out. The problem with it centered on the question of who should collect and allocate the tax or fee, the government, or the radio industry? One method smacked of "socialism", and the other of "private monopoly", with the result being that neither alternative was acceptable to enough people to be adopted. Such a government tax system was used in Britain from 1922 to 1924 to provide additional revenue for the B.B.C., but was abandoned because it gave an advantage to imported equipment.[22]

But the tax plan as well as more exotic ones such as having listeners buy "imaginary tickets" to "radio concerts", were to become superfluous in the light of one station's extraordinary experiment in financing its broadcasting. The station was WEAF in New York City, owned and operated by A.T.&T. WEAF was set up as a "toll" broadcasting station, available for hire to anyone who wished to broadcast to the public. The first "toll" broadcast on WEAF occurred on August 28, 1922, when the Queensboro Corporation, a Long Island real-estate company, broadcast a ten minute talk

concerning the advantages of living in one of its developments,
Hawthorne Courts.[23] A.T.&T. soon adopted, however, a policy that
permitted no direct advertising, but only a brief announcement to
identify the sponsor of any particular broadcast.

Despite the restriction to indirect advertising, the "toll"
broadcasting experiment was a success. "Some 250 firms and individuals had made commercial broadcasts by the end of 1923, and
practically all of WEAF's time on the air was sold for Thursday,
Friday and Saturday evening hours."[24] It is worth noting, however,
that even with this success, the station's revenues in 1923 were
still more than $100,000 less than its operating expenses.[25]

But the fact that WEAF did in fact have any income at all was
in stark contrast to the rest of the broadcasting industry which had
no income whatsoever. It soon became apparent that A.T.&T. had cast
the die for the entire industry. Whereas "at the First Radio
Conference [of industry and government leaders] in Washington, D.C.,
in 1922, the sentiment against advertising had been almost universal,
by the Fourth Conference, in 1925, the idea of advertising had been
generally accepted."[27] As advertising on the air increased markedly,
the "line" between direct advertising and indirect advertising, such
as that done on WEAF, began to wear thin, and before long any hesita-
tions about allowing direct advertising disappeared altogether.

Earlier fears that radio would not be as effective an advertising medium as newspapers and magazines proved to be groundless.
As can be seen in Table II-1, advertisers turned more and more to
broadcasting to advertise their products. Whereas in 1928 radio

Table II-1

Gross Advertising Billings of Newspapers, Magazines, and
Radio Broadcasting, 1928-1945
($ Million)

Year	Total Three Media	Newspaper	%ᵃ Change	% of Total	Maga-zine	%ᵃ Change	% of Total	Radio Broad-cast	%ᵃ Change	% of Total
1928	1001.8	810.0	----	81	177.7	----	18	14.1	----	1
1929	1066.9	847.0	4.6	79	193.1	8.7	18	26.8	90.1	3
1930	982.4	752.0	(11.2)	77	189.9	(1.7)	19	40.5	51.1	4
1931	895.4	681.0	(9.4)	76	158.4	(16.6)	18	56.0	38.3	6
1932	720.0	546.0	(19.8)	76	112.1	(29.2)	16	61.9	10.5	8
1933	649.7	495.0	(9.3)	76	97.7	(12.8)	15	57.0	(7.9)	9
1934	746.3	557.0	13.5	75	116.4	19.1	15	72.9	27.9	10
1935	804.5	588.0	5.6	73	120.8	3.8	15	95.7	31.3	12
1936	913.4	652.0	10.9	71	143.8	19.0	16	117.6	22.9	13
1937	980.9	674.0	3.4	69	165.7	15.2	17	141.2	20.1	14
1938	892.1	601.0	(10.8)	67	141.0	(14.9)	16	150.1	6.3	17
1939	932.6	610.0	1.5	66	151.5	7.4	16	171.1	14.0	18
1940	1004.4	629.0	3.1	62	167.4	10.5	17	208.0	21.6	21
1941	1068.1	650.0	3.3	61	180.5	7.8	17	237.6	14.2	22
1942	1042.6	610.0	(6.2)	59	177.8	(1.5)	17	254.8	7.2	24
1943	1234.3	695.0	13.9	56	232.1	30.5	19	307.2	20.6	25
1944	1359.8	693.0	(0.3)	51	274.9	18.4	20	391.9	27.6	29
1945	1442.2	722.0	4.2	50	308.7	12.3	21	411.5	5.0	29

ᵃ( ) indicates decrease.

Source: Federal Communications Commission, An Economic Study of Standard Broadcasting (Washington, D.C., 1947), pp. 99 and 101.

Gross Advertising
Billings ($ Millions)

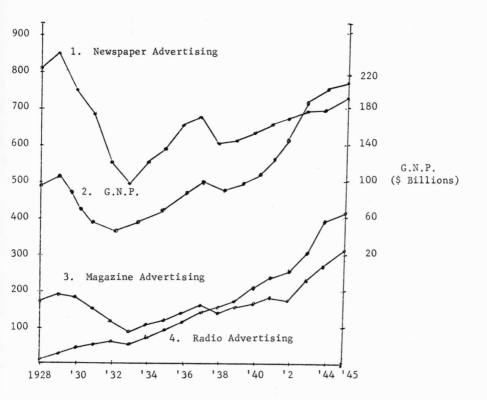

Figure II-1: Trends in Newspaper, Magazine, Radio Billings,
and G.N.P. 1928-1945

Source: Drawn from data in Table II-1; G.N.P.
data from the Economic Report of the President
1973 (Washington, D.C., 1973), p. 193.

accounted for only one percent of the combined gross advertising billings of newspapers, magazines, and radio, by 1945, on the eve of network television, radio had increased its share of the total to twenty-nine percent. Furthermore, those who had argued that advertising would be too unstable a source of income for broadcasting, liable to severe contraction with downturns in the economy, were also proven wrong. It can be seen in Figure II-1 that both newspapers and magazines suffered more from cyclical movements in the economy than did radio. In fact, in the whole period 1928-1945, there was only one year, 1933, in which gross advertising billings of radio declined from the previous year. It is apparent that radio broadcasting had turned out to be an effective "salesman" and advertising a steady source of income.

But if advertising had proven itself to be one leg upon which broadcasting in the United States could stand, networks would soon prove themselves to be the other.

The First Network

The operation of a network, or "chain broadcasting", as it originally was termed, is defined as:

> ... the simultaneous broadcasting of an identical
> program by two or more connected stations. It is
> technically accomplished ... by transmitting the
> program by wire ... from its point of origin to
> each of the outlet stations of the chain or
> network for simultaneous broadcasting. The outlets
> are in certain highly important cases owned by the
> networks themselves, but more commonly they are
> independently owned and are affiliated with the
> networks by means of a network affiliation contract.[28]

With the entrance into radio of advertising, the main objective
of which is to reach as many potential consumers as possible, and
considering the fact that if more than one station could share the
cost of producing programming it would reduce each station's per
program cost, "the trend toward chain broadcasting was irresistible."[29]

A.T.&T. made the first network link-up on January 4, 1923 with a
program broadcast simultaneously over its pioneer New York City
station WEAF, and a Boston station WNAC. The first continuous network broadcasting occurred during the summer of 1923 and consisted of
a three month link-up of WEAF with WMAF in South Dartmouth, Massachusetts. Late in 1923 the Telephone Company inaugurated station WCAP
in Washington, D.C., and it, along with WEAF, became the nucleus of
A.T.&T.'s network. "By the Fall of 1924, the Telephone Company was
able to furnish a coast-to-coast network of twenty-three stations to
broadcast a speech by President Coolidge. At the end of 1925 there
was a total of twenty-six stations on the regular Telephone Company
network, extending as far west as Kansas City."[30]

That networking was in fact more profitable than "toll" broadcasting by individual stations is born out by the fact that for 1925,
its first full year of network broadcasting, A.T.&T.'s broadcast
income "was at last greater than its expense, and its prospect was
one of continuing financial success. The operating profit for 1925
was estimated at $150,000, contrasted with the operating loss of
more than $100,000 for each of the two preceeding years."[31]

Thus, A.T.&T. had proven the viability of the network concept,
but its success had altered the status quo within the radio industry,
and the "radio group" was quick to react.

The Response of the "Radio Group"

The "radio group", sensing that A.T.&T.'s experiments were the wave of the future in radio, was anxious to start "toll" broadcasting and networking itself. Unfortunately, it was prevented from selling time to advertisers, for A.T.&T. claimed that under the cross-licensing agreements of 1920, the exclusive right to sell time for broadcasting purposes, which was after all related to transmitting, and not receiving, equipment, was held by the "telephone group". At first convinced that the Telephone Company had a good legal foundation for its claim, the stations owned by the "radio group" made no charge for the use of their broadcasting time. In addition, A.T.&T. attempted to keep the "radio group" from engaging in chain broadcasting by denying them the use of telephone lines for network purposes.[32]

It soon became obvious that A.T.&T. was out to monopolize radio broadcasting, and as it turns out, such had been the Telephone Company's plan even from the start of its WEAF experiment. In February of 1923, A.H. Griswold, assistant vice-president of A.T.&T. in charge of broadcasting, had told a radio conference open to Bell System executives only:

> ... We have been very careful, up to the present time, not to state to the public in any way, through the press or in any of our talks, the idea that the Bell System desires to monopolize broadcasting; but the fact remains that it is a telephone job, that we are telephone people, that we can do it better than anybody else, and it seems clear ... we have got to do the job.[33]

Despite the hugh obstacle which the Telephone Company's actions and attitudes represented, the "radio group" nevertheless made a start in network broadcasting. R.C.A. acquired control of station WJZ in New York City in the spring of 1923, and made its first network broadcast in December of that year linked to G.E.'s station WGY in Schenectady, New York. The "radio group's" network connections had to be made "with Western Union telegraph wires which were quite inferior for this purpose."[34] So hampered were the "radio group's" operations, that by 1925 A.T.&T.'s network was selling time to advertisers over a basic network of thirteen stations at $2,600 per hour, whereas R.C.A.'s network consisted of only four stations, and was receiving absolutely no income from its operations.[35]

But events were about to make a rapid about-face. The "radio group" had gone to court in an attempt to break A.T.&T.'s monopoly over the sale of broadcasting time. Late in 1925, A.T.&T. sensing a possible unfavorable court decision, and fearful that its telephone monopoly might become endangered, proposed that:

> ... The Telephone Company, for a substantial compensation, agree to withdraw from radio broadcasting and permit the Radio Group to monopolize the field. The Radio Group to secure all of their wire service from the Telephone Company at rates profitable to the Telephone Company.[36]

As a result, on July 1, 1926, a contract was entered into, which became effective November 1, 1926, under which the National Broadcasting Company (N.B.C.), a corporation R.C.A. had formed for this deal, purchased for one million dollars station WEAF and the entire broadcasting business of the Telephone Company.[37] Following the purchase, the only two networks in the country were under the control of R.C.A. The former A.T.&T. network with WEAF as its "flagship" station was renamed the N.B.C. "red" network, and R.C.A.'s own network with WJZ as its "flagship" station was now called N.B.C.'s "blue" network. Although new networks would soon be organized, R.C.A. through its subsidiary N.B.C. was to have a practical monopoly of the radio broadcasting industry for many years to come, and would remain the dominant firm in the broadcasting industry until challenged by another firm upon the advent of television.

The Remaining National Radio Networks

In January of 1927, United Independent Broadcasters was incorporated in New York. The purpose of this company was "to furnish broadcasting programs, to contract for radio time, and to sell time to advertisers."[38] Another company, Columbia Phonograph, along with four private individuals, owned and operated the sales unit of this new network which was known as the Columbia Phonograph Broadcasting System. The first regular broadcast took place on the United network on September 25,1927. Shortly thereafter, United acquired all the outstanding stock of its sales unit, and changed the sales company's name to the Columbia Broadcasting System (C.B.S.). "Subsequently, the sales company was dissolved and United assumed its activities and its name in January of 1929."[39]

The Mutual Broadcasting System (M.B.C.) did not come into being until September 29, 1934, when four stations: WGN in Chicago, WLW in Cincinnati, WXYZ in Detroit, and WOR in New York, agreed to work

jointly to get advertising business for themselves. Organized somewhat differently than previous network companies, stock control of
Mutual was held by two of its stations, WGN and WOR, as well as by
four cooperating regional networks: the Colonial Network, the United
Broadcasting Company (not related to C.B.S.'s predecessor, United),
the Don Lee Network, and the Western Ontario Broadcasting Company,
Ltd.[40]

The last national radio network to come into existence, the
American Broadcasting Company (A.B.C.), was not really new. It came
about when N.B.C. in 1943 sold its "blue" network to a candy manufacturer, Edward Noble. The name, American Broadcasting Company,
was adopted in 1945.[41]

Thus, in 1945, the year before television networking was to
begin, the radio broadcasting industry had a total of four national
networks. But at the same time that advertiser-support, and national
networks, had been developing, another factor had arisen in radio
broadcasting - government regulation.

The Rise of Government Regulation of Broadcasting

The first piece of federal legislation which dealt with the radio
industry was the Radio Act of 1912. Passed in a belated response to
the Titanic disaster, its basic purpose was to prevent unnecessary
interference with radio distress signals. To facilitate this end,
there was included in the act a provision which empowered the
Secretary of Commerce to issue radio station licenses and to specify

the wavelengths to be used.[42] But this licensing power was not anything more than a simple registration procedure since the act

> ...did not provide any grounds on which the
> secretary could reject applications. In the light of
> the limited uses of radio at the time, of course,
> Congress had no particular reason to anticipate that
> the Secretary would need to make any choice.[43]

For nearly ten years, the Radio Act of 1912 was a useful and
sufficient piece of radio legislation. But when broadcasting, as
opposed to point-to-point transmission, began to develop, the act was
not equal to the strain put upon it. Since the Secretary of Commerce
was not empowered to turn down license applications, all available
frequencies were soon used up and more than one station had to be
assigned to many of them. Interference became widespread, and a
marked drop in radio sales resulted.[44]

Secretary of Commerce Hoover, who was opposed to government
regulation in principle, eventually was won over by the industry's
insistence that it wanted and needed federal regulation. With the
public, the industry, and even Herbert Hoover, committed to this
goal, Congress passed the Radio Act of 1927. This new act

> ...provided for a [Presidentially-appointed]
> commission of five members [the Federal Radio
> Commission] with authority to grant, renew or revoke
> station licenses.
> It was definitely established by the act that
> the radio spectrum belonged to the public and that a
> broadcaster acquired no ownership rights when granted
> a license. Before he could be granted a license or a
> renewal of one, he was required to show that the public
> interest would be served. Thus the government was given
> authority to make a systematic assignment of frequencies
> and, within limitations, to set standards and make rules
> for the operation of radio stations.[45]

This act was successful in reducing interference, but certain Congressmen wanted to place all communications, including telephone and telegraph, under the jurisdiction of one "super-agency". This idea gained support with the advent of The New Deal, and so at President Roosevelt's urging, Congress passed the Communications Act of 1934. This new law absorbed the Radio Act of 1927 intact, and added provisions pertaining to wire communications. In addition, two members were added to the regulatory commission, and its name was changed to the Federal Communications Commission.[46]

The basically unchanged Communications Act of 1934 is to the present day the "law of the land" with respect to broadcasting. This means that the theory and practice of federal regulation of broadcasting is essentially unchanged since 1927.

The Extent of Network Power in Radio Broadcasting

As a result of the increasing activity and influence of networks in radio, the Federal Communications Commission (F.C.C.), which had been established by the Communications Act of 1934 "for the purpose of regulating interstate and foreign commerce in communication by wire and radio,"[47] began an investigation of chain broadcasting in 1938. The result of this inquiry was the Report on Chain Broadcasting which the F.C.C. issued in 1941. The major substantive recommendation in the report to have any effect on the industry's structure was that N.B.C. cease its dual network operations, something not finally accomplished until, under increasing government pressure, it sold its "blue" network in 1943.[48]

But despite the government's concern with growing network power
in the radio industry, nothing else was done to stem it. The result
was, that by 1945, as can be seen in Table II-2, the radio networks,
while owning only 29 stations or a mere 3.2 percent of the industry
total, exercised a large degree of control over a total of 706
stations representing over 78 percent of the industry total, through
affiliation contracts. In addition, the most lucrative stations in
the country were owned by existing networks, so that new entry into
networking was extremely difficult without any "superstations"
available to become a "flagship" station for a potential new network.
That the 29 network owned stations were in fact special and deserving
of the term "superstations" is evidenced by the fact that the networks, with only 3.2 percent of the industry's stations, nevertheless,
as Table II-2 also points out, commanded 33.7 percent of broadcasting
revenues, 27.6 percent of broadcasting profits, 16.2 percent of
tangible assets, and accounted for 18.0 percent of employment in the
industry. In addition, network control over the industry's programming was even more extensive, as evidenced by the fact that "in 1945,
approximately 47.9 percent of the time of all standard broadcast
stations was devoted to network programs."[49]

Thus by 1945, the year before television networking began,
network power in radio broadcasting was large. It seemed natural
that the advertiser-support means of financing operations, and
government regulation, would carry over into the developing
television medium. What remained to be seen, was whether this would
lead to the development of network power there as well.

Table II-2

Network Power in Radio Broadcasting-1945

	Four National Networks	Industry Total	Networks as a % of Industry Total
Owned and Operated Stations	29	901	3.2%
Network Affiliates	706	901	78.4%
Broadcast Revenues[a] ($ Million)	101.0	299.3	33.7%
Broadcast Profits[a,c] ($ Million)	23.1	83.6	27.6%
Depreciated Value of Tangible Assets[b] ($ Million)	9.2	56.4	16.2%
Employment[b] (,000's)	7.2	40.3	18.0%

[a]Data for networks and all their owned and operated stations included under Four National Networks.

[b]Data for networks and their 10 "key" owned and operated stations included under Four National Networks.

[c]Before taxes.

Source: Federal Communications Commission, Financial and Employee Data Respecting Networks and Standard Broadcast Stations, 1946 (Washington, D.C., 1947).

FOOTNOTES FOR CHAPTER II

[1]W. Rupert MacLaurin, Invention and Innovation in the Radio Industry (New York: The MacMillan Co., 1949), pp. 12-15.

[2]Erik Barnouw, A History of Broadcasting in the United States, Volume I - to 1933 (New York: Oxford University Press, 1966), pp. 9-15.

[3]Giraud Chester, Garnet R. Garrison, and Edgar E. Willis, Television and Radio (New York: Appleton-Century-Crofts, 1963), p. 21.

[4]Gleason L. Archer, History of Radio to 1926 (New York: The American Historical Society, Inc., 1938), pp. 86-88; Alvin F. Harlow, Old Wires and New Waves (New York: D. Appleton-Century Co., 1936), pp. 454-455.

[5]Chester, et al., Television and Radio, p. 21.

[6]Ibid, p. 22.

[7]Sydney W. Head, Broadcasting in America (Boston: Houghton Mifflin Co., 1956), p. 104.

[8]Barnouw, A History of Broadcasting, I, pp. 57-60.

[9]Quoted in Head, Broadcasting in America, p. 113.

[10]N.R. Danielian, A.T.&T., The Story of Industrial Conquest (New York: The Vanguard Press, 1939), pp. 110-111.

[11]Ibid.

[12]Head, Broadcasting in America, p. 105. (emphasis is Head's)

[13]Quoted in Chester, et al., Television and Radio, p. 23.

[14]Quoted in Archer, History of Radio, p. 112.

[15]Ibid, pp. 202-203.

[16]Chester, et al., Television and Radio, p. 24.

[17] Ibid.

[18] Thomas T. Eoyang, "An Economic Study of the Radio Industry in the United States of America," unpublished Ph.D. dissertation, Columbia University, 1936, p. 84.

[19] Chester, et al., Television and Radio, p. 25.

[20] Barnouw, A History of Broadcasting, I, p. 154.

[21] Quoted in Chester, et al., Television and Radio, p. 25.

[22] Barnouw, A History of Broadcasting, I, p. 157.

[23] William P. Banning, Commercial Broadcasting Pioneer: the WEAF Experiment 1922-1926 (Cambridge, Mass.: Harvard University Press, 1946), p. 150.

[24] Ibid, p. 154.

[25] Ibid.

[26] Danielian, A.T.&T., pp. 120-126.

[27] Head, Broadcasting in America, p. 122.

[28] Federal Communications Commission, Report on Chain Broadcasting (Washington, D.C., 1941), p. 3.

[29] Thomas Porter Robinson, Radio Networks and the Federal Government (New York: Columbia University Press, 1943), p. 18.

[30] F.C.C., Report on Chain Broadcasting, p. 6.

[31] Banning, p. 268.

[32] F.C.C., Report on Chain Broadcasting, p. 7.

[33] Quoted in Danielian, p. 123-124.

[34] F.C.C., Report on Chain Broadcasting, pp. 6-7.

[35] Ibid.

[36] Danielian, A.T.&T., pp. 126-127.

[37] F.C.C., Report on Chain Broadcasting, p. 7.

[38] Robinson, Radio Networks, pp. 26-27.

[39] Ibid.

[40] Ibid, pp. 28-29.

[41] Head, Broadcasting in America, p. 141.

[42] Ibid., p. 156.

[43] Ibid.

[44] Ibid, p. 158.

[45] Walter B. Emery, Broadcasting and Government (East Lansing: Michigan State University Press, 1968), p. 20.

[46] Head, Broadcasting in America, pp. 162-163.

[47] Communications Act of 1934, section I.

[48] Robinson, Radio Networks, pp. 60-74.

[49] Federal Communications Commission, Public Service Responsibility of Broadcast Licensees (Washington, D.C., 1946), pp. 49-50. (Emphasis added)

CHAPTER III

TELEVISION -- THE EARLY YEARS

Although the potential for television broadcasting had been there
for as long as radio broadcasting had been in existence, the more
complex technical problems involved, along with the reluctance of the
F.C.C. to allow "premature" television systems to be foisted upon the
public, resulted in delaying the first commercial television broadcasts until 1941. Then World War II intervened, and it was not until
1945 that television activity once again started to expand. In 1946
the first network television broadcasts took place, and by 1948 the
industry seemed ready to embark on an explosive growth period.
However, a number of problems had arisen as the television broadcasting industry expanded, the most important of which were the
questions of how to allocate the available spectrum space and what
technical standards to adopt for the industry. In order to study
these questions, and be able to issue new rules concerning them, the
F.C.C. stopped processing new license applications in the fall of
1948. This was the beginning of the famous "freeze" which was to last
four years and leave an indelible mark on the structure of the
industry for many years thereafter. Thus the transition from experimental to commercial operations took nearly twice as long in television as it had in radio.

The Scientific Origins of Television

As was the case with radio, early developments which provided the scientific foundations for television were developed by university scientists in Europe. In 1884 a German engineer, Paul Nipkow, invented a scanning disc which made it possible to transmit a reproduction of live moving objects. Nipkow's disk

> was perforated with a single spiral of holes, each hole a little nearer the center than the preceeding one. When the disc was placed directly between a light source and an object and slowly rotated, the light shone through one hole at a time. After one complete turn every element of the object had been illuminated by the narrow beam of light from the lamp. Passing through the holes in the scanning disc and striking the object to be televised, the light next encountered a selenium cell. Each element of the picture was received there separately, and a stream of current variations was sent along a wire to a receiver. At the receiving end Nipkow attempted to reconstruct the picture on a screen by means of a synchronized disc.[1]

Had it worked perfectly, the viewer would have been presented successive scenes at such speed, that due to a peculiarity of the human eye known as "persistence of vision", he would have believed he was seeing continuous action.[2]

In 1889 another German, Lazare Weiller, developed a scanning system similar to Nipkow's. In this new system, however, the scanning disc was replaced by a drum covered with small mirrors which reflected the image being televised, also onto a selenium screen.[3]

But all such systems which depended upon mechanical moving parts were doomed to failure. The slowness of rotation of either the discs or drums involved meant that the picture received was blurry, thus keeping television at the level only of an interesting curiosity.

Nevertheless, much effort went into attempts to promote mechanical

systems in the late 1920's and early 1930's.[3] In fact, Charles F.

Jenkins, an American inventor, produced a crude, but workable,

mechanical system in the late 1920's and

> ...in 1929 the Jenkins Television Company was
> formed to manufacture both transmitting and receiving
> apparatus. Commercial programs were announced for 1930,
> and the Jenkins company licensed a number of manufacturers
> under its patents to make sets. However, before regular
> broadcasting was started, it became obvious that the
> company could not make a profit, and Jenkins Television
> went into receivership.[4]

But meanwhile, a number of scientists were proposing the idea

that an all electronic scanning system was the only way to get

picture definition of reasonable quality to support commercial

operations. Early work on such a device had been done by Professor

Boris Rosing at the St. Petersburg Technological Institute in Russia

in the year 1907.[5] But electronic television was still a long way

from being a reality, and whereas the impetus for radio development

had passed from the universities to individual inventor-entrepreneurs

and only later to large corporations, the development of electronic

television now by-passed that middle stage.

The next major development was the invention in 1928 by Vladimir

Zworykin, a Russian who had emigrated to the United States in 1919,

of a practical photo-electric tube for television transmission.[6] But

Zworykin's invention, which he called the "iconoscope", was made

while he was an employee of a large, established firm in the

electronics industry, Westinghouse. Furthermore, he was employed specifically for the purpose of doing research on an all electronic

television system. In effect, he was the prototype of present day

R. and D. (Research and Development) men utilized in industrial

research by large corporations. In a similar manner, the final

development of an all electronic television system which combined

the iconoscope with a whole series of later, less important, yet

still necessary, refinements, was the result of:

> a systematic attack on all aspects of television
> development, investigating not only technological
> problems, but also the subjective question of
> standards required to win public acceptance of
> television as a regular service...[7]

by a team of engineers, including Zworykin, working for R.C.A. at its

research laboratories in Camden, New Jersey.[8] After almost a decade

of intense work, the system they developed had a successful, large-

scale, public demonstration at the New York World's Fair in 1939, and

television as we know it today was finally born.

The reason small, individual entrepreneurs played a lesser role

in the development of television than in that of radio is apparent if

we look at the figures presented in Table III-1. The major (and a

couple of minor) electronics and radio corporations spent over

$15 million on research and development before an all electronic

television system was perfected. Very few individuals could have

made the expenditures on a "potential" system that these large

companies did, and survived financially. Furthermore, the two

individuals who did make important contributions to the development

of television receivers - Philo Farnsworth and Allen B. DuMont, both

formed companies which made costly research efforts (see Table III-1),

Table III-1

Expenditures on Television Research
and Development Through 1939*

	Company	
1.	American Telephone and Telegraph Co.	$ 3,389,529[a]
2.	Columbia Broadcasting System	1,312,240[b]
3.	Radio Corporation of America	9,253,723[c]
4.	Farnsworth Television, Inc.	1,033.795[d]
5.	Allen B. DuMont Laboratories, Inc.	275,468[e]
	Total	15,264,753

[a]For the years 1925-40.

[b]For the years 1936-39.

[c]For the years 1930-39.

[d]For the years 1929-38.

[e]For the years 1931-39.

*In addition, similar, but unknown, amounts were spent by Philco,
General Electric, Sylvania, and Westinghouse during this same period.

Source: W. Rupert MacLaurin, Invention and Innovation in the Radio
Industry (New York: The MacMillan Co., 1949), pp. 159, 206, 210-211,
217, 220.

that were financed to a large extent by the backing of other, still

larger, corporations, Farnsworth by Philco, and DuMont by Paramount

Pictures.[9]

MacLaurin has summarized best how television developed during

this period as follows:

> Television ... is the type of product which ...
> required long years of applied research and
> advanced engineering to bring it to the commercial
> stage. ... Research expenditures ... [were]
> enormous, ... technical obstacles to be overcome
> were exceedingly difficult, and ... it would be
> many years before sets could be sold in large
> volume. It is not surprising, therefore, to find
> that in the prewar period research contributions to
> television were made primarily by the very large and
> well-established companies.[10]

Experimental Television Broadcasting

Experimental television stations (mostly using mechanical

systems) had been in operation even before the Radio Act of 1927.

The Federal Radio Commission, established by that act, announced in

1928 a future policy of:

> ... allow[ing] a few broadcasting stations to
> experiment with television in the broadcast
> band on their assigned channels on condition
> that this form of communication be limited to a
> small amount of time per day and be so conducted
> as not to cause interference on adjacent channels.[11]

At the same time the Commission also stated that it had not

determined its final policy with regard to television broadcasting.[12]

The Commission during its short existence continued to encourage

experimental telecasting, but in its last report in 1933 observed that, "although much progress has been made in the laboratory, visual broadcasting is still in the experimental stage."[13]

In 1934, the Federal Communications Commission, created by the Communications Act of that year, inherited the guardianship of the experimental television situation. Things progressed slowly as before, but with R.C.A.'s successful World's Fair demonstration of electronic television in 1939, the F.C.C. suddenly found itself with a number of applications "requesting the use of television frequencies as a public service." This was in contrast to previous authorizations, "which were primarily directed toward the development of equipment standards and systems of transmission."[14]

As a result, the F.C.C. set up a special committee to "study the various aspects of television and to recommend to the Commission a policy which might serve as a guide to the industry."[15] The committee's first report, issued in May of 1939, recognized that the F.C.C. faced "a most complex problem of engineering, economics, and sociology," and recommended caution on the part of the Commission lest "premature decisions ... which might later prove to hamper the orderly development of the industry" be made "by administrative fiat to freeze the art at this stage of its development." The committee also proposed that "cooperative coordination between the manufacturers of receiver apparatus, the operators of licensed transmitting stations, and the Federal Communications Commission might be desirable in the development of television as a national service in the interest of the public."[16]

In effect the F.C.C. was being counseled to continue the period
of experimental broadcasting, but industry pressures were mounting to
commercialize the new medium. R.C.A., which had spent over nine
million dollars on television research and development (see Table III-
1), requested that the F.C.C. relax its rules banning commercial
sponsorship of programs on experimental television stations. But the
F.C.C., sticking to its avowed position of maintaining orderly development of television broadcasting service, denied the request in
November of 1939, stating:

> Since only a few experimental stations in operation
> today are rendering broadcast service to not more than
> 1,000 receivers, there is no convincing argument that
> the removal at this time of the ban on commercialization
> will affect the development of television in any positive
> manner.[17]

But industry pressure for commericalization, now coming from
C.B.S., Philco, DuMont and others, as well as from R.C.A., was becoming intense. As a result, "on February 29, 1940, the Commission
issued a report and order which permitted 'limited commercialization'
beginning on September 1, 1940." Perhaps feeling that R.C.A. and
C.B.S.'s dominance of commercial radio would spill over into
television, the Commission emphasized that station licenses "were
still experimental ... and full commercialization would not be
permitted until 'genuine and healthy competition' in television could
be assured."[18]

The F.C.C. soon realized, however, that it had erred even in
this first tentative step towards allowing the commercialization of

television. Its mistake involved what has been called the "lock

and key" relationship of television transmission and reception. As

Sydney Head points out:

> ... the television receiver [unlike the radio
> receiver] must do more than detect and amplify
> the television signal. It must also carry out
> the precisely timed scanning sequence in exact
> synchronism with the camera. Unless both
> transmitter and receiver operate on the same
> line and field frequencies, and unless the
> receiver is designed to receive and interpret
> specific synchronizing signals, the key will not
> fit the lock.[19]

The F.C.C. in deciding to allow limited commercial operations

had not adopted uniform technical standards for television trans-

mitters and receivers. Its reasoning seems to have been that to do

so might "freeze" television technology at this primitive level,

since the public would acquire a strong vested interest in maintaining

the system of standards which fit the equipment they had already

purchased in this period of limited commercialization. What the

F.C.C. failed to see, but which became apparent when R.C.A. began a

marketing "blitz" to sell its television apparatus before the

commercial operations commenced, was that a de facto set of

standards, based upon the system used by the company selling the most

apparatus, might easily come into being.[20]

Realizing its error, the Commission withdrew its decision to

allow limited commercialization in May of 1940. But in the face of

certain industry protest, it promised approval of "full commercial-

ization as soon as the engineering opinion of the industry is

prepared to accept any one of the competing systems of television

broadcasting as the standard system." Again, however, the Commission
stated its commitment to a television system "organized so as to
provide genuine and healthy competition within an unfettered industry"
and not a "mere semblance of competition."[21] In order to "eliminate
the possibility that the standards might be influenced by one manufacturer more than by another, a new industry-wide committee of
engineers, the National Television System Committee (N.T.S.C.), was
set up to recommend standards."[22]

Commercial Television Broadcasting Begins

Nearly one year later, on May 3, 1941, the F.C.C. announced the
technical standards (based largely on proposals of the N.T.S.C.)
which were to be adopted for the television industry. Full commercial
operation was to be authorized on eighteen very high frequency (V.H.F.)
channels, each six megacycles wide, located between 50 and 294 megacycles on the broadcasting spectrum band. In addition, television
stations would broadcast 525 line pictures at a speed of 30 frames
per second.[23] These standards provided for the transmission of black
and white pictures only, despite C.B.S.'s contention that color
television was already technically feasible.[24]

The first stations to get commercial licenses were two experimental ones owned by the leading radio networks, N.B.C.'s station
W2XBS (now to be known as WNBT) in New York City, and C.B.S.'s
station W2XAB, also in New York. Both commenced commercial operations
on July 1, 1941.[25] Numerous other companies applied for new commercial licenses or to have their experimental station licenses

converted to commercial ones. But before much work could be done on

building new stations, manufacturing television receivers on a large

scale, or experimenting with programming, World War II intervened.

As a result, "on April 22, 1942, all production on such civilian

goods as radio and television sets came to a halt."[26] And whereas

World War I, through the federal government's rationalizing of the

chaotic radio industry, speeded up the development of commercial

radio broadcasting, World War II substantially delayed the develop-

ment of commercial television. The reason for this is quite simple.

Whereas radio was seen as an essential communication service for a

war effort, television (at least in 1942) was seen as a superfluous

service needing to be curtailed in order to free spectrum space for

more critical needs. Not surprisingly, while in May of 1942, ten

commercial television stations had been on the air and several others

were under construction, by September of 1944 only six stations were

still functioning, and even these were on severely curtailed broad-

casting schedules of four hours per week.[27] These pioneer stations,

in addition to the New York stations of N.B.C. and C.B.S. which were

still operating, were: another N.B.C. station, W3XPP in Philadel-

phia; another C.B.S. station, W9XAB in Chicago; a station owned by

Allen B. DuMont Laboratories, Inc., WABD in New York; and one owned

by Don Lee Broadcasting, Inc., W6XAO in Los Angeles.[28]

The Post-war Confusion

The F.C.C., anticipating a post-war expansion of commercial

television broadcasting, on August 15, 1944, scheduled a general allocation proceeding to determine the needs of nongovernmental services for frequencies in the broadcast spectrum.[29] One of the thorniest problems to be resolved was just where in the spectrum commercial television should be located. In the previous section it was noted that television broadcasting was authorized on eighteen V.H.F. channels between 50 and 294 megacycles in the broadcast spectrum. But World War II had greatly expanded government, particularly military, demands for frequencies in this portion of the spectrum. The result was that after the war the F.C.C. felt it could make only thirteen channels available to commercial television in the V.H.F. band. Partially as a response to this situation, one group of industry spokesmen, led by C.B.S., "contended that the best place for television was in the Ultra High Frequency (U.H.F.) band (between 480 and 890 megacycles)," where more spectrum space was available.[30] But an opposing group, including N.B.C. and DuMont, felt that commercial television should continue in the V.H.F. They argued "that the use of the U.H.F. involved operating difficulties the solution of which would require extensive research and experimentation; and that many years might elapse before a U.H.F. system could be established."[31] In May of 1945, the Commission, fully realized that there was "insufficient spectrum space below 300 megacycles to make possible a truly nationwide and competitive television system."[32] Still it was reluctant to affect adversely the interests of the television pioneers in the V.H.F. band. Accordingly it made the first in a series of compromise decisions which were to

contribute heavily to the eventual non-competitive industry structure
which it had stated it wished to avoid. The decision was that
commercial television could go ahead on the thirteen[33] available
V.H.F. channels, but in addition the Commission assigned 480 to 890
megacycles in the U.H.F. band to experimental television. It noted
that ultimately it expected television to be located in this upper
frequency "where color pictures and superior monochrome (black and
white) pictures can be developed through the use of wider channels."[34]

Contrary to the Commission's expectations, its decision and the
subsequent resumption of station licensing did not lead to a great
upsurge in television activity. Part of the problem was that the
post-war economy had many materials shortages which prevented a
large scale resumption of manufacturing television transmitters and
receivers. But perhaps more important was the Commission's own
equivocating position concering the U.H.F. versus V.H.F. and color
versus black and white controversies. Since the two positions in
each controversy seemed incompatible (at least from the technological
viewpoint of the mid-forties), a choice between them would eventually
have to be made. And as Sydney Head points out, "In the meantime,
manufacturers and potential station licensees, unwilling to risk
betting on the wrong horse, preferred to wait for clarification of
the issue."[35]

The issue was brought to a head in September of 1946 when C.B.S.
filed a petition with the F.C.C., again requesting approval of
commercial color television broadcasting in the U.H.F. band.[36]
Despite the massive publicity which C.B.S. had given its color

system, it became clear during the Commission's hearings on the request, which included demonstrations, that color television was far from being perfected, and that C.B.S.'s system was "limited in its potential quality in terms of brightness, freedom from flicker, and fidelity."

On March 18, 1947, the F.C.C. denied C.B.S.'s petition.[37] This decision, although providing for further experimentation in color and U.H.F. broadcasting, seemed to remove much of the hesitancy on the part of those considering entrance into the television field. In addition, the post-war materials shortages were ending, and whereas only 6,476 television receivers had been produced in 1946, over 178,000 were built in 1947.[38] All things considered, the time seemed ripe for a "take-off" period in the television industry.

The Rise of Television Network Interconnection

Unlike the interconnection of radio networks which took place via telephone wires, or even in some cases via telegraph wires, the interconnection of television networks required special cables[39] built for this purpose. As early as 1936 the F.C.C. had authorized the construction by A.T.&T. of coaxial cables between New York and Philadelphia, "to be used in part for the experimental transmission of television signals."[40] On November 9, 1937, the first television pictures and sound were transmitted over the newly installed cable. After several experimental broadcasts over the cable in 1938 and 1939, in June of 1940 the Republican National Convention was televised in Philadelphia and transmitted to New York via the cable for broadcast there.[41] By the end of 1941, additional cables had been built between

Washington, D.C. and Baltimore, and between Baltimore and Philadel-

phia, but the expansion stopped there with the onset of World War II.[42]

Even before the war had ended, A.T.&T. petitioned the F.C.C. to

build additional cable facilities between New York and Washington, D.C.,

because C.B.S., N.B.C., and DuMont had "inquired of the American

Telephone and Telegraph Co. regarding the possibility of providing

facilities for the transmission ... of television programs between

such points as New York and Washington [which] would be a material

step forward in the development of future television networks."[43]

In July of 1945, the F.C.C. authorized construction of the new

cable, but with the proviso that it was to be used:

> ... only for purpose of experimentation and no
> commercial use thereof is hereby authorized' ...
> and ... unless and until further authorization
> is granted by the Commission upon appropriate
> application, no charges shall be made by the
> applicants for the use of the facilities
> authorized herein for television transmission
> service.[44]

On February 12, 1946, the newly completed cable was inaugurated

with an experimental broadcast of Lincoln Memorial services from

Washington, D.C. to N.B.C., C.B.S., and DuMonts' stations in

New York.[45] This date is commonly referred to as the birthdate of

television network broadcasting, despite the facts that experimental

interconnection had taken place earlier, and that this was still

considered an experimental link-up by the F.C.C. Broadcasts over

the cable multiplied rapidly, but still only by the three companies

mentioned previously. Between November of 1946 and April of 1947, there were only 34 days on which neither N.B.C., C.B.S., nor DuMont made use of the facilities. Therefore in July of 1947, A.T.&T. requested authorization from the F.C.C. to begin commercial operation of its television cable facilities. Such authorization was granted on February 12, 1948, and commercial network television broadcasting was ready to begin.[46]

The F.C.C. and the Nascent Television Networks

During all or part of 1947, fifteen television stations were in operation, and 54 more permits to construct new stations were granted.[47] At least seven companies were contemplating the establishment of television networks. They included the four national radio networks, N.B.C., C.B.S., A.B.C., and Mutual, two manufacturers of radio and television equipment, DuMont and Philco, and one motion picture company, Paramount Pictures. The fact that these companies were trying to form networks was never construed by the F.C.C. as being counter to its policy of fostering competition in television broadcasting. Accepting advertiser-support as a fait accompli in the American system of broadcasting, the Commission had repeatedly pointed out:

> ... that the 'high cost' of program production for television, in order to be economically feasible, must be spread over a large number of stations and communities through interconnection. ... [and] that networks of generally the same type as had grown up in radio would be relied upon to assume the responsibilities for national interconnected service. ... [but since] radio experience had taught that a national system of broadcast communication, based upon advertising support

and operated through interconnection, is
centripetal in tendency. ... the Commission
plac[es] prime importance on avoidance of
dominance at the national level[48] [presumably
this refers to the position two networks,
N.B.C. and C.B.S., held in radio].

Thus the "competition" envisioned by the F.C.C. seems always to have

been that between a relatively small number (e.g. six or seven) of

networks, but with no one or two of them clearly stronger than the

rest. It has always meant then oligopolistic competition. Further-

more, the Commission seems to have planned on (and whether this was

realistic from the standpoint of conventional oligopoly theories is

certainly questionable) the number, and equal strength, of the oligo-

polistic competitors to ensure performance in the public interest.

Given the normalizing of the post-war economy, and the F.C.C.'s

relatively "final" decision regarding the U.H.F. and color questions,

combined with its benign attitude toward networks, it should come as

no surprise that in 1948 a rush to stake out national television

networks began. But as this rush began, the field of entries quickly

diminished. Of the radio networks, Mutual, due to lack of financial

resources, dropped its television network plans early in 1948. For

similar reasons, one manufacturer, Philco, also dropped out at about

the same time. Paramount Pictures, although not officially dropping

its network plans, did little more than operate two stations. Thus

by the middle of 1948 it became obvious that the "genuine and healthy"

competition which the F.C.C. had hoped for in television, would at

best be limited to four networks: N.B.C., C.B.S., A.B.C., and DuMont.

Although fewer than the number the Commission had originally en-

visioned, the F.C.C. still had hopes that the industry would be

competitive if no one or two of the networks reached a position of
dominance in the television field. To prevent this from happening,
the Commission had, from the start of commercial operations, limited
the number of television stations allowable to any one owner to five.
However, with such a rule in effect, the route to power in the
industry now shifted to the process of affiliation.

Network Affiliation Begins

Stations' affiliation with networks had come about first in
radio, due to the advertiser-support nature of American broadcasting.
Affiliation can be described as the process in which "a network
company secures contracts with a number of geographically dispersed
stations for access to their frequencies, and in turn the network
sells to advertisers time in which to convey ... commercial messages
over the entire 'network' of stations." The network in effect acts
as "a brokerage office to bring national advertisers, the buyers,
into contact with dispersed licensed television stations, the
sellers, for the purpose of utilizing the stations' broadcasting
time."[49]

Affiliation contracts work to the benefit of both stations and
networks. The network usually receives about 70 percent of the
proceeds of time sales to advertisers. Every new affiliate increases
the size of its potential audience, thus raising the price it can
charge advertisers per time period of its programming. The local
station involved, while only receiving about 30 percent of the time
sale proceeds, nevertheless, is relieved of the financial burden of

supplying programming, and the task of finding sponsors, for those
time periods when it "clears" (i.e. accepts for broadcast) network
offerings.[50] In addition, the local stations sell spot announcement
time before and after programs, and this time usually is work more
to advertisers if it is adjacent to a network, rather than to a
locally originated, program.[51] Affiliation has strong attractions
for both stations and networks. The only question which remains is
with which network will any particular station choose to affiliate?

As 1948 began, there were 19 commercial stations on the air. Of
these, 9 belonged to or were affiliated with N.B.C., one was owned by
C.B.S. which had no other affiliates as yet, two were owned by DuMont
which had no other affiliates, and as of then A.B.C. neither owned nor
had any affiliated stations on the air.[52] At this point then, N.B.C.,
the leading radio network, had clearly gotten off to the best start
in building a television network.

By the end of 1948, 50 stations were on the air, and the
affiliate situation had changed accordingly. N.B.C. now had 24
affiliates, C.B.S. now led the pack with 28, DuMont had 14, and A.B.C.
had 20.[53] If we add up the affiliates, we get more stations than were
on the air, but this oddity is explained by the fact that except for
the stations owned and operated by the networks themselves; very few
others affiliated exclusively with any one network. Thus they had an
added advantage of a selection of network offerings from which possibly
to choose programs to clear. Although comparative clearance figures
are not available, the fact that many of the fifty stations on the
air were owned by persons or firms that also owned radio stations

which were exclusively affiliated with N.B.C. or C.B.S. tended to
make television station clearances of their programs much more likely
than for DuMont or A.B.C. programs. While the networks jockeyed for
position in the industry, the public "discovered" television.

Expansion Begins, Then is Frozen

As noted earlier, 50 stations were on the air in 1948. In
addition, permits had been granted, or applications filed, for over
100 more stations. The public, responding to increased viewing
opportunities, started buying more and more television sets. Factory
production for 1948 was over 1,000,000 sets, more than five times the
number that had been produced in 1947.[54] Furthermore, whereas cable
interconnection had only existed on the Eastern seaboard in January
of 1948, during the year such facilities had been extended to Pittsburgh, Cleveland, Buffalo, Toledo, Detroit, Chicago, Milwaukee, and
St. Louis.[55] With the expanding network interconnection, "important
advertisers began experimenting with the new medium and large-scale
programming began - the national political conventions, Milton
Berle's Texaco Star Theatre, Ed Sullivan's Toast of the Town,
[etc.]."[56]

But by the fall of 1948, the F.C.C. realized:

> ... that the current allocation plan, adopted
> before a great deal was known about V.H.F.
> propogation, resulted in interference between
> stations; and the twelve channels then
> allocated to television were going to be
> entirely inadequate to take care of the demand
> for stations. Furthermore, the color question
> which had clouded the question all along became
> more and more pressing as the technology of the
> medium progressed.[57]

As a result of these problems, the Commission called a meeting with industry representatives on September 13-14, 1948, at which time it was announced that an engineering conference to consider revision of the Commission's rules and standards would be called. Pending the outcome of this conference, the F.C.C. "by its order of September 30, 1948 (the 'freeze' order) called a halt in the processing of applications for new television stations. It was thought that the 'freeze' could be lifted within six to nine months," but events would prove otherwise.[58]

Concentration and Performance During the Early Years

The theory presented in Chapter I which predicted a divergence between private and public performance in television broadcasting was based upon the assumption that the industry was an oligopoly. In order to decide whether any industry should be structurally classified as an oligopoly, it has to be determined whether the largest firms in that industry have a share of the market large enough "that they will recognize the interaction of their own behavior and their rivals' response in determining the values of the market variables."[59] One commonly used measure of the relative size of market shares is the concentration ratio, defined as the percentage of some total indicator of market activity (e.g. sales, profits, etc.) accounted for by a specific number of the largest firms in the industry.

However, as Carl Kaysen and Donald F. Turner have pointed out, "neither economic theory nor experience provides a definite number of firms, or a size of market share they must jointly hold," for the

classification of industries as either oligopolistic or not.[60]
Nevertheless, they adopted as a dividing point a market share of one
third of the total market for the eight largest sellers. They felt
that those markets with a smaller number of firms with larger shares
of the market generally exhibit the type of behavior described above
for structural oligopolies.[61] Although they admitted that their
dividing point was purely arbitrary, it has been adopted to a large
extent in later studies in the field of industrial organization, and
will be used in this examination of the television broadcasting
industry.

The concentration ratios which will be used in this study are,
for the years 1948-1954, four-firm ratios representing the share of
the total market accounted for by the four national networks. For
the years 1955-1956, the ratios are three-firm, due to the reduction
in number of national networks from four to three. The ratios
computed will include the familiar ones concerning share of industry
revenues, profits, assets, and operating units (in this case stations).
In addition, ratios of network affiliated, and exclusive network
affiliated, stations to the total number of stations in the industry
will be computed. These are relevant ratios because the extent of
network influence on the industry's programming is the direct result
of the extent of network affiliation.

Data for the television industry in the years 1946 to 1948 are
rather scant, and no trends were clearly discernible. Looking at
Table III-2, we can see that the total number of stations was
increasing more rapidly than the number of those owned by the

Table III-2

Network Concentration in Television Broadcasting
1946-1948

Year	Total Sta- tions	Net- work Owned	% of Total	Net- work Affili- ated	% of Total	Indus- try Reve- nues[a]	Net- work Reve- nues[a]	% of indus- try	Indus- try Pro- fits[a]	Net- work Pro- fits[a]	% of indus- try
1946	10	3	30.0%	n.a.	n.a.	.7	n.a.	n.a.	n.a.	n.a.	n.a.
1947	15	5	33.3%	n.a.	n.a.	1.9	n.a.	n.a.	n.a.	n.a.	n.a.
1948	50	10	20.0%	43	86.0%	8.7	4.8	55.2%	(14.9)	(6.4)	43.0%

[a]In millions of dollars, ( ) denotes loss.

n.a. - not available

Source: Federal Communications Commission, Broadcast Financial Data for Networks, and AM, FM and Television Stations, 1947, 1948 (Washington, D.C., 1948, 1949).

networks. This fact, combined with the F.C.C.'s rule on multiple-
ownership meant that the station ownership concentration ratio would be
a poor measure of network influence in the industry. The radio had declined to twenty percent in 1948, and would continue downward in future
years. A much better indicator of network influence is the ratio of
network affiliated stations to the total number of stations. Although
this figure for 1948 is a high 86 percent, it probably overstates the
networks' influence over the industry's stations at this point in time,
since these stations were not for the most part, as affiliates would
become in later years, exclusive affiliates of any one network. And
furthermore, a sample of stations taken by Television magazine in
November of 1948 would seem to indicate that stations' clearance of
network programming was not very extensive, averaging about 39 percent of total programming.[62] Another indicator of network concentration is the percentage of total industry revenues which accrued to
the networks either from the income of their owned and operated stations, or from their share of their affiliates' revenues. As also can
be seen in Table III-2, in 1948, the first year for which such
data are available, the networks received 55.2 percent of all industry
revenues. The networks' share of the industry's gross profits will
also be used as an additional concentration indicator. In 1948,
again the first year in which such data are available, the entire
television broadcasting industry was operating at a loss, and the
network absorbed 43.0 percent of this total loss. Thus although the
few concentration ratios which can be computed for 1948 do
indicate that the networks' share of the total market may already have

been higher than 30 percent, the data are too sparse to make a firm

conclusion, and certainly no trend can be ascertained.

Concerning private performance in the years 1946-1948, although

no profits were made by either the networks or the industry as a

whole, it must be remembered that this was essentially a starting-up

period. In such a period investment (and thus costs) are tradition-

ally high as many fixed capital expenditures must be made, while

revenues may be low as buyers must be sought out and "sold" on a new

product (in this cast television programming). Thus it is too early

to make any judgment concerning private performance or to try and

relate such performance to the level of network concentration.

Turning now to public performance, again little can be seen. In

later periods data on network and industry program expenditures will

be examined as tentative indicators of program quality, but such data

are not available for this early period.

In an attempt to test the theory presented in Chapter I which

predicted that the diversity component of public performance would

suffer in an oligopolized broadcasting industry, four indices have

been set up to measure different aspects of television program

diversity. Two of these indices, Index #1 and Index #3, were set

up to measure overall program diversity. They will show whether the

average number of different program types (irrespective of whether

these were types which appealed to audiences with "mass appeal " or

"specialized appeal" tastes) offered increased, decreased, or stayed

the same as the network oligopoly developed. These overall indices

are computed from two different time perspectives, Index #1 being a quarter-hourly index, and Index #3 being a daily index. This was done because there is some question as to whether viewer satisfaction depends on the number of program choices offered at every time period during the day (quarter-hour time periods were chosen because in the forties and fifties many shows were only 15 minutes in length), or on the number of choices offered during the viewing day as a whole.

However, since the theory in Chapter I specifically predicts that it would be "specialized appeal" programs which would not be broadcast by a network oligopoly, two indices were set up to measure "specialized appeal" program diversity. These indices, Index #2 and Index #4, will show whether the average number of "specialized appeal" program types offered increased, decreased, or stayed the same as the network oligopoly developed. As with the overall indices, Index #2 and Index #4 are calculated from a quarter-hourly, and daily, time perspective respectively.

The method of computing each index and its range of possible values is set out in the Appendix. Since indices #1 and #3 reflect diversity among all program types, including the "specialized appeal" types reflected in indices #2 and #4, one would expect that the values of Index #1 and Index #3 would always be higher than the values of Index #2 and Index #4 respectively (except in the unlikely event that all programming broadcast was "specialized appeal" programming).

In order to determine whether station programming might have offset any trends which might develop in network programming, the four diversity indices were also computed for the program schedules

offered in the Chicago and New York markets. These cities were

chosen because in all the years of this study except 1948, Chicago

had at least as many stations as there were national networks, and

New York had several more stations than there were national networks.

Before 1948, no reliable program schedules are available, so

diversity could only be examined for the year 1948. As can be seen

in Table III-3, the program schedules of the four national networks

in operation in 1948 yielded a value for Index #1 of 1.96, for

Index #2 of 1.20, for Index #3 of 10.0, and for Index #4 of 5.71.

Since there are no earlier years with which to compare them, one

cannot even speculate as to a trend in network program diversity.

The most that can be said is that as expected, Indices #2 and #4, the

"specialized appeal" diversity indicators, are lower in value respec-

tively than Indices #1 and #3, the overall diversity indicators.

Looking at the diversity in programming in the Chicago market,

in 1948 (when Chicago had only three stations, one less than the

number of networks), all four indices are lower in value than for

the networks.

Looking at the diversity in programming in the New York market,

in 1948 (when New York had six stations, two independents and four

network affiliates), three of the four indices are higher than for

the network program schedules.

It should be noted that the indices for the networks, and the

Chicago and New York markets as well, contain a downward bias due to

Table III-3

Television Program Diversity -- 1948

Market	O.A.Q. Index #1	S.A.Q. Index #2	O.A.D. Index #3	S.A.D. Index #4
Networks	1.96	1.20	10.00	5.71
Chicago	1.71	.90	8.43	4.43
New York	2.85	1.74	10.14	5.71

Note: O.A.Q. - Overall quarter-hourly diversity indicator.
       S.A.Q. - "Specialized appeal" quarter-hourly diversity
              indicator.
       O.A.D. - Overall daily diversity indicator.
       S.A.D. - "Specialized appeal" daily diversity indicator.

Source: See Appendix.

the fact that no station or network sampled was broadcasting a full

prime-time schedule of programs during 1948.

Thus as the early years of television ended in 1948, television

broadcasting was a small (total revenues were a mere three percent of

those for radio in 1948[63]), unprofitable, and with the "freeze" in

effect - confused, industry. As yet no trends were discernible in

either concentration or performance.

FOOTNOTES FOR CHAPTER III

[1]W. Rupert MacLaurin, Invention and Innovation in the Radio
Industry (New York: The MacMillan Co., 1949), p. 192.

[2]Ibid.

[3]Ibid, pp. 192-193.

[4]Sydney W. Head, Broadcasting in America Second Edition (Boston:
Houghton Mifflin Co., 1972), pp. 186-188.

[5]MacLaurin, Invention and Innovation, p. 224.

[6]Ibid, p. 202.

[7]Head, Broadcasting in America Second Edition, p. 190.

[8]Ibid.

[9]Ibid, p. 189; MacLaurin, Invention and Innovation, p. 224.

[10]MacLaurin, Invention and Innovation, p. 224.

[11]Federal Radio Commission, Second Annual Report (Washington,
D.C., 1928), pp. 21-22.

[12]Ibid, p. 22.

[13]Federal Radio Commission, Seventh Annual Report (Washington,
D.C., 1933), p. 31.

[14]Federal Communications Commission, Fifth Annual Report (Washington, D.C., 1939), p. 45.

[15]Ibid.

[16]Federal Communications Commission, Release No. 34168, May 22,
1939, quoted in Federal Communications Commission, Second Interim
Report by the Office of Network Study - Television Network Program
Procurement, Part II (Washington, D.C., 1965), pp. 142-143.

[17]Federal Communications Commission, Release No. 37460, November 15, 1939, quoted in F.C.C., Second Interim Report, Part II, p. 147.

[18]Federal Communications Commission, Release No. 41662, February 29, 1940, quoted in F.C.C., Second Interim Report, Part II, p. 151.

[19]Head, Broadcasting in America Second Edition, p. 185.

[20]Ibid, p. 192.

[21]Federal Communications Commission, Release No. 41249, May 28, 1940, quoted in F.C.C., Second Interim Report, Part II, p. 152.

[22]Head, Broadcasting in America Second Edition, p. 193.

[23]U.S. House of Representatives, Committee on Interstate and Foreign Commerce, 85th Congress, 2nd Session, Network Broadcasting - Report of the Network Study Staff to the Network Study Committee of the Federal Communications Commission (Washington, D.C., 1957), p. 18.

[24]Head, Broadcasting in America Second Edition, p. 193.

[25]F.C.C., Second Interim Report, Part II, p. 153.

[26]Head, Broadcasting in America Second Edition, p. 193.

[27]U.S. House, 85th Congress, 2nd Session, Network Broadcasting, p. 18.

[28]U.S. Senate, Committee on Interstate and Foreign Commerce, 85th Congress, 2nd Session, Allocation of T.V. Channels - Report of the Ad Hoc Advisory Committee on Allocations (Washington, D.C., 1958), p. 41.

[29]U.S. House, 85th Congress, 2nd Session, Network Broadcasting, p. 18.

[30]Ibid.

[31]Ibid.

[32]Ibid.

[33] In 1947, the F.C.C., in order to provide more spectrum space for land-mobile and other communication services, reduced television broadcasting's allocation of V.H.F. channels to twelve.

[34] U.S. House, 85th Congress, 2nd Session, Network Broadcasting, p. 19.

[35] Head, Broadcasting in America Second Edition, p. 193.

[36] U.S. House, 85th Congress, 2nd Session, Network Broadcasting, p. 20.

[37] Ibid, pp. 20-21.

[38] Television Factbook, Number 27, Fall-Winter 1958, p. 28.

[39] The system of cables was later supplemented by microwave relay facilities.

[40] F.C.C., Second Interim Report, Part II, p. 158.

[41] Ibid, pp. 158-159.

[42] Ibid, p. 159.

[43] Ibid.

[44] Ibid.

[45] Ibid.

[46] Ibid, pp. 151-162.

[47] Television, Volume IV, Number 12, December, 1947, p. 3.

[48] F.C.C., Second Interim Report, Part II, p. 150.

[49] Robert W. Crandall, "The Economic Effect of Television-Network Program 'Ownership'," Journal of Law and Economics, October, 1971, p. 386.

[50] U.S. Senate, Committee on Interstate and Foreign Commerce, 84th Congress, 1st Session, Investigation of Television Networks and the UHF and VHF Problem - Progress Report Prepared by Robert J. Jones, Special Counsel (Washington, D.C., 1955), pp. 20-21.

[51] S.M. Benson and R. Soligo, "The Economics of the Network-Affiliate Relationship in the Television Broadcasting Industry," American Economic Review, Volume LXIII, Number 3, June, 1973, p. 261.

[52] F.C.C., Second Interim Report, Part II, pp. 166-182.

[53] Ibid.

[54] Television Factbook, Number 27, Fall-Winter 1958, p. 28.

[55] F.C.C., Second Interim Report, Part II, p. 162.

[56] Head, Broadcasting in America Second Edition, p. 194.

[57] Ibid.

[58] U.S. House, 85th Congress, 2nd Session, Network Broadcasting, p. 22.

[59] Carl Kaysen and Donald F. Turner, Antitrust Policy, An Economic and Legal Analysis (Cambridge, Massachusetts: Harvard University Press, 1959), p. 27.

[60] Ibid.

[61] Ibid.

[62] Television, Volume V, Number 11, November, 1948, p. 6.

[63] Federal Communications Commission, Broadcast Financial Data for Networks and AM, FM, and Television Stations, 1948 (Washington, D.C., 1949), mimeo - no page numbers.

CHAPTER IV

TELEVISION -- THE "FREEZE" YEARS

Although the end of 1948 found the television broadcasting industry frozen at its then current level of operation, both the F.C.C. and the industry were optimistic that the "freeze" would last less than a year. Unfortunately, the number of different problems which were to come under consideration, combined with a reticence on the part of the Commission to make another "final" decision which might soon have to be revised, postponed the planned early lifting of the "freeze". The final "thaw" was postponed until April of 1952, nearly four years after the "freeze" had first been imposed. What happened during these four years, particularly to the relative strengths of the four networks, profoundly affected the final structure which would emerge in the industry.

The "Freeze" Begins

Hearings concerning station interference and to determine the utility of the U.H.F. band for commercial broadcasting were held by the F.C.C. late in 1948. After a variety of testimony from industry and government sources, "several months later, in July of 1949, the Commission set out proposed television standards and a nationwide assignment plan. The Commission invited ... industry comments on its proposals."[1]

These comments were swift in coming and generally critical in nature. The most controversial part of the Commission's proposed decision was the plan to intermix V.H.F. and U.H.F. station

allocations in the same markets. The F.C.C. felt this was necessary
in order that every community in the country be within the signal
range of at least one station.[2] This principle of complete local
coverage, while sounding rather democratic and perhaps even pro-
competitive to those unfamiliar with the economics of commercial
television broadcasting, was realized to be totally unsound by the
industry itself.[3] The problems with both inter-mixture and complete
local coverage stemmed from the advertiser-support nature of
commercial broadcasting, and affected both individual stations and
networks. As was noted in Chapter I, it is the number of potential
customers which their commercial messages might reach, which determines the price advertisers will pay for programming on any given
station. Given the facts that in 1949 virtually no television sets
were equipped to receive U.H.F. signals, and that U.H.F. transmitters
developed lower-power (and therefore, shorter distance) signals than
their V.H.F. counterparts, the potential circulation of U.H.F.
stations would be extremely small. This would put these stations
at a decided disadvantage vis-a-vis V.H.F. stations in competeting
for advertisers in the same markets. Thus many critics maintained
that the U.H.F. allocations in the F.C.C.'s plan were mere "phantom"
stations, with little chance of being applied for, or if getting on
the air, with little chance of ever being profitable. In addition,
by spreading the available station allocations thinly over the
entire geographical area of the country, very few large metropolitan
areas could have as many as four V.H.F. stations.[4] The result of this
would be that not all four of the existing television networks could

obtain the station outlets in major markets which were needed in order
to survive. This was crucial because advertisers who bought network
programming time, like advertisers who bought station programming
time, were concerned with the number of potential consumers their
commercial messages would reach. Without affiliates in all the major
metropolitan markets, the programs of A.B.C. and DuMont would have
much smaller circulations than those of N.B.C. and C.B.S. Thus it
seemed likely that the two weaker networks would not be able to
compete effectively for advertisers' business under the proposed
allocation plan.

In response to the F.C.C.'s seemingly short-sighted proposal,
the DuMont organization (which had no radio network as did A.B.C.,
and thus stood to lose its place in broadcasting altogether) submitted its own nationwide allocation plan about a month after the
Commission's had been unveiled.[5] As a Senate Ad Hoc Advisory
Committee was to note later:

> The DuMont project was exemplary for its breadth
> of understanding of the problem and for its professional
> quality. ...[It] took into account economic consider-
> ations, ...[and] saw with lucidity the fatal dangers of
> intermixture.
> ...The plan faced realistically the vital inter-
> relationship of stations and networks and the importance
> of competition between the networks themselves. It
> yielded a minimum of four channels, either U.H.F. or
> V.H.F., not intermixed, in most of the major metropolitan
> markets. ...There was but one intermixed city among the
> first 325 in market rank.[6]

The principle of non-intermixture can not be emphasized enough,
for had the F.C.C. adopted it, manufacturers would have had an
incentive to produce television sets with the capability of receiving

U.H.F. signals for sale in those cities with such allocations
exclusively. In contrast, with intermixed markets, these same
manufacturers, who were doing quite well making V.H.F.-only sets,
were unwilling to invest time and money developing U.H.F. sets until
they saw that the U.H.F. stations would survive against their V.H.F.
competitors.[7] Such survival was impossible without U.H.F. receivers
in the hands of the public, and so the whole problem was circular,
and seemingly unsolveable, in nature.

But the Commission reacted coldly to DuMont's proposed plan.
The reason for this probably is not that the F.C.C. was trying to
lessen competition or destroy the two smaller networks (which would
have been antithetical to its previously stated goals for the
industry), but rather that it was once again unwilling to affect
adversely existing interests in the industry, and had chosen to
compromise instead. Thus the seemingly irrational allocation plan
was actually the result of a completely rational (at least from the
Commission's standpoint) decision:

> ...not to disturb existing V.H.F. stations. There
> were some 90 V.H.F. stations on the air and 19 construc-
> tion permits in effect at the time. Intermixture,
> consequently, was inevitable. The task as executed by
> the Commission then was to build out the national
> structure to the extent the 12 V.H.F. channels would
> permit, then chink up the cracks with U.H.F.[8]

In contrast, DuMont, as a potential competitor, not a sensitive
regulator, had proposed "changing 20 on-the-air V.H.F. stations to
U.H.F. and changing 29 other V.H.F. assignments to U.H.F. to achieve
the appropriate degree of non-intermixture."[9]

The Commission had set September 26, 1949, as the date for hearings to begin on its allocation proposal, but abandoned this schedule when the color controversy once again rose to the forefront.

The Color Television Hearings

In the fall of 1949, considerable interest had once again developed in color television. At least three companies, including C.B.S., claimed to have perfected color systems. As a result, members of the Senate Interstate and Foreign Commerce Committee, particularly its chairman, Edwin C. Johnson of Colorado, expressed the view that "if color were here, this was a crucial fact and every effort must be made to foster its acceptance."[10] The Commission, in large part bowing to Congressional pressures, postponed its scheduled allocations hearing and began instead a color television hearing in September of 1949. When it started "it was estimated that the proceeding might last about three weeks. In fact, it lasted a year and provoked bitter controversy."[11]

As the color hearing proceeded into early 1950, pressures were mounting to end the "freeze". Areas of the country without television were clamoring for the new medium. Congressmen from these "blacked-out" areas questioned why the allocations problem could not be settled separately from the color controversy, or at least temporary stations be allocated to those areas with none at all. Prominent television critics such as Jack Gould of The New York Times accused the F.C.C. of being "at the beck and call" of Senator Johnson who wanted the color controversy settled before the freeze was lifted.[12] A.B.C. and DuMont argued that unless new allocations were

made soon, allowing them to obtain more affiliates, their networks

would go under. A frustrated Allen B. DuMont charged melodramatic-

ally in February of 1950:

> There are ...men [referring to Senator Johnson
> and the members of the F.C.C.] whose refusal to face
> reality has mired television in a rainbow-hued swamp
> that can soon have our industry on its knees.[13]

The Commission's response to all these pressures to end the

"freeze" was exemplified by the comments of its chairman, Wayne Coy,

in a speech made in Portland, Oregon on May 19, 1950:

> ...The kind of standards we set for the V.H.F.
> and the U.H.F. might tie our hands with regard to
> future color. We might be ruled by the dead hand of
> the past. ... Also, to begin making piecemeal
> allocations would not be calculated to insure the
> stability of what should be one of America's greatest
> industries.[14]

Finally on September 1, 1950, the Commission issued its first

color television report, finding the C.B.S. system the best of those

available, but withholding final adoption because of its incompatibi-

lity with existing black and white equipment.[15] Despite this

problem, the F.C.C., one month later on October 10, 1950, adopted the

C.B.S. system.[16] Thereupon R.C.A., strongly supported by most of the

other manufacturers, stations, and networks in the industry, filed a

court suit against the F.C.C. ruling that delayed the actual start

of the C.B.S. system until May 28, 1951, when the Supreme Court of

the United States upheld the F.C.C. in the matter.[17] As Sydney Head

notes, however, "conveniently C.B.S. was saved from the necessity of

facing the final test of its color system in the market," because the

Korean War intervened and the Office of Defense Mobilization asked

manufacturers not to make color receivers and equipment (which

utilized certain "essential" war materials which black and white

sets did not).[18] The final resolution of the color controversy did

not come until after the "freeze" ended. But after it made its

disputed color decision in October of 1950, the F.C.C. resumed its

hearing on television station assignments and engineering standards,

and so by the end of 1950, allocations once again assumed the center

stage.

The Allocation Problem Revisited

After hearing testimony on intermixture, on reserving alloca-

tions for educational television, and on problems of interference and

station separations, the Commission issued what is known as its

Third Notice on March 21, 1951.[19] The station assignment plan in this

new proposal was little different from the F.C.C.'s 1949 plan. It

included both the most objectionable parts of the earlier plan -

intermixture and complete local coverage in station allocations. As

in 1949, an opportunity was given for industry comments. The only

formal response was from DuMont once again, which realizing that:

> ...the Commission was insisting on intermixture,
> ...undertook to salvage its work [on allocations]
> through the medium of a modified plan, alternative
> and, it believed, also superior to the Commission's.
> The alternate plan was designed still to permit four
> or five networks to operate. The plan differed from
> the Commission's plan in that it continued to recog-
> nize the relatively underdeveloped status of U.H.F.
> and therefore assigned four or more V.H.F. channels
> to as many of the major markets as possible.[50]

But the F.C.C., no more receptive to this than to the previous
DuMont effort, rejected the alternate plan and instead, on April 11,
1952, issued its "master plan" for television, the famous Sixth
Report and Order.[21] The station assignment table was basically what
had been laid out in the Third Notice, and in the body of the Sixth
Report and Order were as noted the Commission's objections to the
DuMont alternate plan. Although conceding that in many respects the
DuMont plan was similar to its own, the Commission nevertheless, felt
that:

> A basic objective of the DuMont assignment plan is
> to provide major metropolitan centers with multiple
> V.H.F. stations. In particular, DuMont seeks the
> assignment of four V.H.F. channels to such communities –
> an objective related to DuMont's contention that this is
> necessary to promote network competition.
> ...The Commission has taken into account other
> significant factors. ...[It] finds that the principles
> of assignment which DuMont advocates are inadequate in
> that these principles do not recognize specifically
> the need to provide an equitable apportionment of
> channels among the separate States and communities and
> ...[therefore] the Commission ...has attempted to provide
> at least some V.H.F. channels to each of the states
> although in some cases this was done where an assignment
> might otherwise have been made to a large metropolitan
> center in an adjacent State.[22]

This reasoning, which seems to have been politically motivated
(to avoid criticism by members of Congress from less populous states),
rather than economically justified, led a noted television engineer,
Stuart L. Bailey, to comment that "for the first time in television
history square miles [are given] priority over people in the assignment of channels."[23]

With the issuance of the Sixth Report and Order, the F.C.C.
lifted the "freeze" on new station allocations effective July 1, 1952.

Despite the official end of the "freeze", there was a backlog of

station applications to be processed, and some materials shortages

caused by the Korean War. As a result, only 14 stations, in addi-

tion to those operating or authorized before the "freeze" started,

got on the air before the end of 1952.[24]

Network Developments During the "Freeze"

As 1948 ended, there were 50 stations on the air. Before the

"freeze" order took effect, 58 permits for other new stations had

been issued, and so construction of these stations was allowed to

continue, and they were allowed to take to the air, even during the

"freeze". How this situation affected the four existing networks

was effectively summarized in the testimony presented by Allen B.

DuMont before a Senate Subcommittee on Communications in 1954:

> The 108 stations which were on the air or which
> went on the air shortly after the freeze [began] were
> situated in 63 markets - 40 of these 63 markets had
> only one station; 11 of these 63 markets had only
> two stations; 8 markets had only three stations and
> 4 markets had four or more stations. Of the 40 stations
> in the single station markets, 37 were owned by interests
> having radio stations. As overwhelming majority of them
> were affiliated with [the] N.B.C. and C.B.S. radio
> networks and these affiliations were carried over into
> affiliation with these two television networks. Of the
> 22 stations in the two station markets, 21 were owned
> by radio interests with an overwhelming majority of these
> having affiliations with N.B.C. and C.B.S.[25]

That so   of the pre-freeze station allocations went to interests

already affiliated with the N.B.C. and C.B.S. radio networks seems to

fit the pattern of allocation behavior on the part of the F.C.C.

predicted in Chapter I. The resulting situation, as DuMont continued:

> ...meant that the freeze reserved to two networks
> the almost exclusive right to broadcast in all but 12
> of the 63 markets which had television service. It
> meant that the other two networks did not have ...more
> than a ghost of an opportunity to get programs into
> the markets so necessary ...to ...attract advertisers
> from whom revenues and profits must come.[26]

Although, as for earlier years, comparative program clearance

figures are not available for the four networks, the breakdown of

advertisers' expenditures presented in Table IV-I bears out DuMont's

assessment of the dominance of N.B.C. and C.B.S. in this area during

the "freeze" years. Advertisers' expenditures are usually directed

to those stations or networks with the largest circulations, and

without adequate numbers of affiliates to clear one's programs a

network cannot make much claim to high national circulation. The

fact that C.B.S. and N.B.C.'s network billings were from two to four

times greater than A.B.C. or DuMont's in this period, leads to the

conclusion that the former two networks had a decided advantage over

the latter two in program clearances.

In addition to the rather dismal revenue picture depicted in

Table IV-I, A.B.C. and DuMont faced problems with the cost side of

their situations as well. During the "freeze" years, A.T.&T. had

completed its transcontinental link of coaxial cables and had added

much of the nation in between to the system as well.[27] The rates it

charged the networks for the use of this interconnection service

came under two typical plans - contract and occasional use. The

contract rate was $39.50 per month per mile for eight consecutive

hours of audio and video relay per day, for seven days a week. This

was in contrast to the occasional rate which was $1.15 per hour per

Table IV-I

Television Network Billings[a] 1949-1952
($ Millions)

	Total Network Billings	N.B.C.	% of Total	C.B.S.	% of Total	A.B.C.	% of Total	DuMont	% of Total
1949	12.3	6.5	53%	3.4	28%	1.4	11%	1.0	8%
1950	45.3	21.2	47%	13.0	29%	6.6	15%	4.5	10%
1951	128.0	59.2	46%	42.5	33%	18.6	15%	7.8	6%
1952	180.8	83.2	46%	69.1	38%	18.4	10%	10.1	6%

[a]Network billings, which are not exact revenue figures due to discounts, etc., are nevertheless, accepted by the networks themselves, and by the industry generally, as a satisfactory index of comparison and trends.

Note: Individual network's billings may not add up to the industry total, nor their percents of the total to 100, due to rounding.

Source: Publishers' Information Bureau estimates appearing in Television Factbook, Number 23, Fall-Winter 1956, p. 26.

mile per day. Thus if an occasional user (such as DuMont or A.B.C.

which only cleared a couple of hours of programming a day with all

their potential affiliates) bought two hours a day for a month, the

monthly charge would amount to $69.00 a month per mile.[28] DuMont

and A.B.C. protested to the F.C.C. that A.T.&T.'s rate structure was

discriminatory and a violation of the antitrust laws, but the Commis-

sion took no action.[29] In addition to the burden of price discrimina-

tion, DuMont was also required by A.T.&T. to purchase the same extra

audio facilities as did C.B.S., N.B.C., and A.B.C. for their radio

networks, despite the fact that DuMont had no such network. DuMont's

protest to the F.C.C. in this matter also went unheeded.[30]

It seems clear that network development during the "freeze"

years had resulted in the dominance of the four member oligopoly by

those firms which had earlier dominated radio - N.B.C. and C.B.S.

But despite the obstacles to expansion of their operations which

A.B.C. and DuMont faced, in some ways the term, "freeze" years, is

a misnomer when applied to the television industry in the years

1949-1952.

Industry Growth During the "Freeze" Years

The only facet of the industry which was badly retarded by the

"freeze" was station building, and even there, the number of stations

on the air more than doubled from 50 to 122 from 1949 to 1952.

Factory production of television sets steadily climbed from the figure

of 1,000,000 sets in 1948 to over 6,000,000 sets in 1952.[31] Whereas

at the end of 1948 only .4 percent of American homes had television sets, by the end of 1952 34.2 percent had them.[32] Furthermore,

television broadcasting was beginning to catch up to its predecessor,

radio. By the end of 1952, annual television revenues were 70 per-

cent as large as those for radio, compared with a figure of only 3

percent as large in 1948.[33] Television, despite the "freeze", had

been a growing industry in the period 1949-1952, and as it grew, so

did network concentration.

Concentration and Performance During the "Freeze" Years

With more data available for the period 1949-1952 than for the

period 1946-1948, certain trends which were visible in the earlier

period, appear for the first time in the "freeze" years. In

Table IV-2, it can be seen that although the number of network owned

stations had increased to 15 by 1952, this still represented a

decreasing portion, now only 12.3 percent, of the total number of

stations in the industry. But as was mentioned in Chapter III, the

F.C.C.'s multiple ownership limitation makes this figure a poor

indicator of network concentration in television broadcasting. A

better indicator of such concentration, also appearing in Table IV-2,

is network affiliation. By 1952, 95.1 percent of all stations were

network affiliated. Of course, as was also mentioned in Chapter III,

this figure tends to overstate the networks' horizontal economic

power since many of these stations were simultaneously affiliated

with more than one network. For that reason, it might be useful to

look at the figure for stations which were affiliated exclusively

with one network, also appearing in Table IV-2. The number of these

Table IV-2

Network Station Ownership and Affiliation 1949-1952

	Total Stations	Network Owned	% of Total	Network Affiliated	% of Total	Exclusive Affiliates	% of Total
1949	98	14	14.3%	92	93.9%	28	28.6%
1950	107	14	13.2%	101	94.4%	35	32.7%
1951	108	15	14.0%	102	94.4%	43	39.8%
1952	122	15	12.3%	116	95.1%	44	36.1%

Source: Compiled from the data on television industry's present status appearing in the December issues of the magazine Television in the years 1949-1952.

exclusive affiliates increased slowly from 28 in 1949 to 44 in 1952, and in the latter year represented 36.1 percent of all stations in the industry. But there is reason to suspect that while total affiliation figures tend to overstate network influence, exclusive affiliation figures tend to understate such influence. The reason for such a suspicion is, as noted in Chapter III, that a sample of network affiliates (most of which were non-exclusive) yielded an average figure for clearance of network programs of about 39 percent in 1948. It is quite likely that in the period 1949-1952 this clearance figure had climbed even higher because of the practice, engaged in to a large degree by N.B.C. and C.B.S., and to a much smaller degree by A.B.C. and DuMont, known as "option time".[34] This practice involved a clause included in network affiliation contracts that specified the number of hours per day which the affiliated station had to clear for network programs if the network was able to sell the time to advertisers.

The whole procedure was at the "option" of the network. If he could sell a certain period of time even up until just before air time, the affiliate had to clear that time period for the network program. Conversely, if an advertiser should at the last minute cancel an order for time during option hours, the network would cancel its clearance request and the affiliate would then have the double burden of providing local programming in the time period, and having to make a last minute time sale to a local advertiser. It may seem that the network was getting all the benefit from the option time arrangement, but stations were loathe to give up affiliation with a major network which provided them high-cost, audience-appealing programming free, and in addition shared the revenues with them from network time sales of option hours. In order to get their affiliates to clear as many prime-time hours as possible, the contracts were arranged so that for a certain minimum number of option time hours (which affiliates were required to agree to in order to keep their affiliation) all proceeds went to the network. After the minimum was reached, however, as the number of option time hours a station cleared increased, he was given a correspondingly increasing share of the total proceeds. The result was that stations were under strong pressures from both the cost and revenue side of their budgets to clear most, if not all, of the prime-time program schedules of one of the major networks, even if they were not exclusive affiliates.

Some further indicators of network concentration during the "freeze" years are presented in Table IV-3. It can be seen in this table, that during the entire period, over 50 percent of industry revenues accrued to the networks. The networks' share of the industry's gross profits, also presented in this table, is in 1951, the first year the industry as a whole is not operating at a loss, 26.4 percent. The following year, the network profit share dips to 17.8 percent, but this may be an interruption in any trend which may eventually develop caused by the extraordinary expenses incurred by the networks in broadcasting the 1952 Presidential Conventions. Figures on the industry's assets, available for the first time in 1949, show a steadily increasing network share which stood at 54.7

Table IV-3

Television Industry Revenues, Profits, and Assets 1949-1952
($ Millions)

	Industry Revenues	Network Revenues	% of Industry	Industry Profits[a]	Network Profits[a]	% of Industry	Industry Assets[b]	Network Assets	% of Industry
1949	34.3	19.3	56.3%	(25.3)	(12.1)	47.4%	44.9	14.7	32.7%
1950	105.9	55.5	52.4%	(9.2)	(10.0)	108.7%	50.3	18.0	35.8%
1951	235.7	128.4	54.5%	41.6	11.0	26.4%	63.2	26.8	42.4%
1952	324.2	180.2	55.6%	55.5	9.9	17.8%	84.8	46.4	54.7%

[a]Before taxes.
[b]Depreciated value of tangible broadcast property.

Note: ( ) denotes loss.

Source: Federal Communications Commission, Broadcast Financial Data for Networks and AM, FM and Television Stations, 1949, 1950 (Washington, D.C., 1950, 1951). Federal Communications Commission, Final TV Broadcast Financial Data 1951, 1952 (Washington, D.C., 1952, 1953).

percent in 1952. Thus almost every indicator of network concentration examined for the period 1949-1952 shows an already large, and
in some cases increasing, share of the market in the hands of the
network oligopoly. If one examines performance figures for the same
period, an attempt can be made to relate such performance to the
apparent trend network concentration in the industry.

Neither the industry nor the networks operated profitably
before 1951, but the figures on rates of return presented in
Table IV-4 indicate that when the turning point came, the improvement in private performance was dramatic. The 1951 rates of return
of 65.8 percent and 41.0 percent for the industry and the networks,
respectively, are handsome indeed. The fact that the private
performance of the networks is not as good as for the industry as a
whole is due to the continued losses of A.B.C. and DuMont. In 1952,
the rate of return for the industry remains at its high level, but
the dip in network profits explained previously, cuts their rate of
return almost in half. Thus as network concentration increased
during the "freeze" years, private performance took a rapid turn for
the better, although no trend in this performance was as yet discernible.

Turning now to public performance, it can be seen in Table IV-5,
that figures for program expenditures, which are used as indicators
of the quality component of public performance, indicate that the
networks consistently outperformed the rest of the industry during
the "freeze" years. By 1952, the networks accounted for 7.10 percent
of all industry program expenditures. In addition the networks
consistently spent a larger part of their total expenditures on

Table IV-4

Television Industry Rates of Return 1949-1952

	Industry Assets[a]	Industry Profits[b]	Rate of Return[c]	Network Assets[a]	Network Profits[b]	Rate of Return[c]
1949	44.9	(25.3)	----	14.7	(12.1)	----
1950	50.3	(9.2)	----	18.0	(10.0)	----
1951	63.2	41.6	65.8%	26.8	11.0	41.0%
1952	84.8	55.5	65.4%	46.4	9.9	21.3%

[a]Depreciated value of tangible broadcast property ($ Millions).

[b]Before taxes ($ Millions).

[c]Ratio of before-tax profits to depreciated value of tangible broadcast property.

Note: ( ) denotes loss.

Source: Federal Communications Commission, Broadcast Financial Data for Networks and AM, FM and Television Stations, 1949, 1950 (Washington, D.C., 1950, 1951).   Federal Communications Commission, Final TV Broadcast Financial Data, 1951, 1952 (Washington, D.C., 1952, 1953).

Table IV-5

Television Industry Program Expenditures 1949–1952
($ Millions)

	Total Program Expenditures	Network Program Expenditures	Network % of Total	Total All Expenditures	Network All Expenditures	Industry Program % of All Industry Expenditures	Network Program % of All Network Expenditures
1949	n.a.	n.a.	n.a.	n.a.	n.a.	n.a.	n.a.
1950	59.8	40.0	66.9%	115.1	65.5	52.0%	61.1%
1951	109.1	75.6	69.3%	194.1	117.4	56.2%	64.4%
1952	150.6	106.8	71.0%	268.7	170.3	56.0%	62.7%

Source: Federal Communications Commission, Broadcast Financial Data for Networks and AM, FM and Television Stations, 1949, 1950 (Washington, D.C., 1950, 1951). Federal Communications Commission, Final TV Broadcast Financial Data 1951, 1952 (Washington, D.C., 1952, 1953).

programming than did the industry as a whole. Thus if program expenditures are some indication of program quality (and they may only be a necessary, and not sufficient factor contributing to such quality), then this component of public performance was favorably affected by increasing network concentration in the industry during 1949-1952.

Concerning the diversity component of public performance, it can be seen in Table IV-6 that for network programming, Index #1, the indicator of quarter-hourly overall program diversity, increased from a value of 2.21 in 1949 to a value of 2.74 in 1952. But the trend in Index #3, the indicator of daily overall program diversity, is unclear, since it drops in value from 11.86 in 1949 to 10.00 in 1950, and then increases in value to 11.29 in 1952. The most likely explanation of this is that the networks, as rational oligopolistic competitors, were most interested in differentiating their products (programs) at different time periods during the day when viewers actually made their choice of which network program to watch, rather than being interested in the total number of different program types available over the whole day since that would have little effect on viewers' decisions at any particular time period within that day. Looking at Index #2 and Index #4, the "specialized appeal" diversity indicators, it can be seen that their values in all years are, as expected, lower than those for overall program diversity. Although no trends are noticed, the 1952 value of .88 for Index #2, and 4.86 for Index #4, are lower than the respective values of 1.16 and 6.29 for the year 1949. Thus as the networks' horizontal economic power

Table IV-6

Television Program Diversity 1949-1952

Networks

	O.A.Q. Index #1	S.A.Q. Index #2	O.A.D. Index #3	S.A.D. Index #4
1949	2.21	1.16	11.86	6.29
1950	2.65	.86	10.00	3.86
1951	2.73	1.00	10.86	4.71
1952	2.74	.88	11.29	4.86

Chicago

	O.A.Q. Index #1	S.A.Q. Index #2	O.A.D. Index #3	S.A.D. Index #4
1949	2.92	1.37	13.29	7.29
1950	3.36	1.36	12.71	6.00
1951	3.29	1.37	13.71	6.71
1952	3.37	1.44	13.00	5.86

New York

	O.A.Q. Index #1	S.A.Q. Index #2	O.A.D. Index #3	S.A.D. Index #4
1949	4.33	1.99	13.86	7.00
1950	4.81	1.95	13.71	6.29
1951	5.01	2.39	14.57	6.86
1952	4.86	2.41	14.29	7.00

Note: O.A.Q. - Overall quarter-hourly diversity indicator.

S.A.Q. - "Specialized appeal" quarter-hourly diversity indicator.

O.A.D. - Overall daily diversity indicator.

S.A.D. - "Specialized appeal" daily diversity indicator.

Sourse: See Appendix.

increased, their program schedules reflected an increasing overall program diversity at each time period, but apparently only a diversity among "mass appeal" program types.

If one now looks at the values of these indexes for Chicago, which had four exclusive network affiliated stations during this entire period, the situation is quite interesting. Although no trends are discernible, Index #2 is higher in value in 1952 than in 1949, the opposite of the situation for the network program schedules. In addition, although the values of the other three indexes are different and in the same direction as the network schedules in 1952 compared to 1949, in all cases they are higher in value than the respective indexes for network programming. This would seem to indicate that station programming (even by exclusive network affiliates) is more conducive to diversity than is network programming, particularly with regard to "specialized appeal" programs.

Looking now at the values of these indexes for New York, which had four exclusive network affiliates and three independent stations throughout the "freeze" years, there are some similarities to the Chicago situation. Index #1, as for the networks and Chicago, is higher in value in 1952 than in 1949, but at a higher level than either the networks or Chicago throughout the period. Index #2 increases from 1.99 in 1949, to 2.41 in 1952, despite having dropped to a value of 1.95 in 1950. Index #3, despite also dropping off in 1950 is at 14.29 in 1952 versus 13.86 in 1949. And Index #4 after dropping from 7.00 in 1949 to 6.29 in 1950, rises to a value of 7.00 by 1952. It seems then that all diversity indexes, including

those for "specialized appeal" programming were positively affected
by the number of stations in a market as well as the factor of
station versus network programming. Thus as network concentration
in the television broadcasting industry increased during the "freeze"
years, station programming remained largely impervious to the trend
(if indeed it was a trend) towards decreased "specialized appeal"
program offerings in the network program schedules.

By the time that the "freeze" years came to an end in 1952,
television broadcasting had expanded appreciably, had become profitable, and had seemingly gotten its future course finally charted in
a "master plan" drawn up by the F.C.C.

What the increasing network concentration which had developed
during these years portended for future performance both public and
private was still unclear. Similarly unclear was whether the four
member oligopoly would continue to be totally dominated by N.B.C.
and C.B.S. Both these uncertainties would be finally resolved in
the "post-freeze" years, 1953-1956.

FOOTNOTE FOR CHAPTER IV

[1] U.S. House of Representatives, Committee on Interstate and Foreign Commerce, 85th Congress, 2nd Session, Network Broadcasting - Report of the Network Study Staff to the Network Study Committee of the Federal Communications Commission (Washington, D.C., 1957), p. 24.

[2] Ibid.

[3] U.S. Senate, Committee on Interstate and Foreign Commerce, 85th Congress, 2nd Session, Allocation of T.V. Channels - Report of the Ad Hoc Advisory Committee on Allocations (Washington, D.C., 1958), pp. 98-100.

[4] Ibid.

[5] Ibid, p. 98.

[6] Ibid, pp. 98-99.

[7] John M. Kittross, "Television Frequency Allocation Policy in the United Stated," unpublished Ph.D. dissertation, University of Illinois, 1959, p. 309.

[8] U.S. Senate, 85th Congress, 2nd Session, Allocation of T.V. Channels, p. 99.

[9] Ibid.

[10] U.S. Senate, 85th Congress, 2nd Session, Network Broadcasting, p. 24.

[11] Ibid, p. 25.

[12] Quoted in Kittross, "Allocation Policy," p. 253.

[13] Quoted in Television Digest, Volume VI, Number 6, February 11, 1950, pp. 1-2.

[14] Quoted in Kittross, "Allocation Policy," p. 254.

[15] U.S. House, 85th Congress, 2nd Session, Network Broadcasting, p. 25.

[16] Ibid.

[17] Ibid.

[18] Sydney W. Head, Broadcasting in America Second Edition (Boston: Houghton Mifflin Co., 1972), p. 200.

[19] U.S. House, 85th Congress, 2nd Session, Network Broadcasting, p. 26.

[20] U.S. Senate, 85th Congress, 2nd Session, Allocation of T.V. Channels, p. 100.

[21] U.S. House, 85th Congress, 2nd Session, Network Broadcasting, p. 26.

[22] U.S. Senate, 85th Congress, 2nd Session, Allocation of T.V. Channels, p. 100.

[23] Quoted in Kittross, "Allocation Policy", p. 244.

[24] U.S. House, 85th Congress, 2nd Session, Network Broadcasting, pp. 30-31.

[25] U.S. Senate, Committee on Interstate and Foreign Commerce, Subcommittee on Communications, 83rd Congress, 2nd Session, Hearings on Status of T.V. Stations and S. 3095 (Washington, D.C., 1954), p. 1018.

[26] Ibid.

[27] U.S. House, 85th Congress, 2nd Session, Network Broadcasting, p. 29.

[28] Ibid, pp. 543-544.

[29] Ibid, pp. 544-546.

[30] Gary N. Hess, "An Historical Study of the DuMont Television Network," unpublished Ph.D. dissertation, Northwestern University, 1960, p. 140.

[31] Television Factbook, Number 27, Fall-Winter 1958, p. 28.

[32]Ibid, p. 27.

[33]Ibid, p. 24.

[34]"Option time" was forbidden in network affiliation contracts by the F.C.C. in 1963, on the grounds that it was a "monopolistic practice."

CHAPTER V

TELEVISION -- THE "POST-FREEZE" YEARS

The years following the "freeze", 1953-1956, witnessed the
television industry's attainment of its present market structure.
Given the station allocation plan contained within the F.C.C.'s
Sixth Report and Order, most observers felt it was only a matter of
time before either A.B.C. or DuMont, or both networks, would go out
of business. The Commission was under strong attack from both
industry and Congressional critics concerning its handling of the
U.H.F.-V.H.F. problem and the problem of network competition. The
Senate and the House planned to conduct investigations of these
problems, and the F.C.C. planned to hold an inquiry of its own.
But the one factor, which more than anything else, determined the
shape which the television broadcasting industry's structure would
take, was the F.C.C.'s 1953 decision to allow a merger between
A.B.C. and United Paramount Theatres, Inc. This decision in effect
sacrificed the DuMont network in order that at least A.B.C. might
survive and prosper to offset the obvious dominance which N.B.C.
and C.B.S. had gained in the industry during the "freeze" years.

When the struggling DuMont network ceased operations in
September of 1955, the F.C.C. was well on the way to realizing its
long-held goal of having equal-powered ologopolistic competitors in
television broadcasting. Unfortunately, there were only three such
competitors, which while pushing private performance to new heights

of excellence, at the same time doomed television programming to

becoming, as a future F.C.C. chairman would phrase it - "a vast

wasteland."

The Immediate "Post-freeze" Developments

The most obvious developments in television after the "freeze"

had ended were pleasing to the public. First, a plethora of new

stations appeared. By the end of 1953, 334 stations were on the air,

compared to the 122 at the end of 1952. In addition, television sets

were found in 55.8 percent of American homes, compared to a figure of

44.8 percent in 1952. By the end of 1953, these figures had again

increased to 410 stations on the air, and 64.5 percent of homes with

television sets.[1]

Second, the color controversy was finally settled when on

December 17, 1953, the F.C.C. threw out the C.B.S. system adopted

back in 1951, but which had never gone into large scale production

because of the Korean War. In its place, with the concurrence of

C.B.S., the Commission adopted a system that had been advocated by

R.C.A. and others which was compatible with black and white trans-

mission as well.[2] Although "adoption of color standatds in 1953

did not produce an immediate changeover, ... since color receivers

cost several times as much as monochrome sets," the public was

generally pleased with the knowledge that color television was

finally here.[3] Yet despite a ready and willing public, and the

"networks ... [making] substantial new investments to be able to

originate and transmit color programs, ...a dozen years [would pass]
before color began to turn the corner."[4]

Notwithstanding the public's approval of television expansion
and its enthusiasm over the small amount of color programming already
reaching the air, all was not well in the industry.

Problems with the U.H.F.

The 226 stations which had gone on the air since the "freeze"
ended in 1952, represented 67.8 percent of all the television
stations on the air at the end of 1953.[5] Unfortunately, of the
$432.7 million in total revenues which the industry garnered in
1953, only $26.5 million, a mere 6.1 percent of the total, went to
this large percentage of "post-freeze" stations.[6] Even worse,
whereas the "pre-freeze" part of the industry made $78.5 million
in profits in 1953, the "post-freeze" stations operated at a combined
loss of $10.5 million.[7] Worst of all, from the standpoint of the
F.C.C.'s principle of intermixture, over 60 percent of this loss was
absorbed by U.H.F. stations.[8] The results of all this were, that in
1954, although 25 additional U.H.F. stations went on the air, 29
U.H.F. stations which had started in 1953 ceased operations.[9] This
trend of more U.H.F. stations stopping rather than starting operations
each year continued with 9 starts but 27 stops in 1955, and 6 starts
but 14 stops in 1956.[10] Just as DuMont had predicted as far back as
in 1949, U.H.F. stations could not compete with V.H.F. stations in
the same markets. As the U.H.F. portion of the industry contracted,
those geographical areas which had been allocated U.H.F. stations in

the F.C.C.'s "master plan" started complaining to Congress about
their lack of television service. Politicians once again began to
scrutinize the television industry. In May and June of 1954, a
Communications Subcommittee of the Senate Interstate and Foreign
Commerce Committee held hearings on the U.H.F. problem.[11]

Among the proposed solutions to the problem which were being
publicly discussed at the time were: 1. to move all television
broadcasting to the U.H.F. band so that no stations would have a
competitive advantage, 2. to "de-intermix" selectively those markets
where the problem was most acute, 3. to declare a new "freeze" until
a revised allocation plan could be worked out, 4. to remove the
federal excise tax on all television sets produced which were capable
of U.H.F. reception.[12] Only the last of these proposals had widespread industry support. As the hearings progressed, U.H.F. station
operators and the A.B.C. and DuMont networks pressed hardest for
Congressional action, while N.B.C. and C.B.S. became more and more
defensive. The U.H.F. operators accused the two big networks of
trying to "kill off" the U.H.F. stations by withholding affiliation
contracts from them. A.B.C. and DuMont accused N.B.C. and C.B.S.
of "monopolizing" the V.H.F. affiliates, leaving only the unprofitable
U.H.F. affiliates to carry A.B.C. and DuMont's programs. In defense,
N.B.C. and C.B.S. claimed that they would lose money be extending
affiliation to U.H.F. stations. Doing so would substantially increase
interconnection charges, but without much of an offsetting increase
in circulation, and therefore, in revenues. Furthermore, they
argued, they were not responsible for A.B.C. and DuMont's lack

of viable affiliates since all stations were free to affiliate with
whichever network they wished.[13]

Despite all the testimony which the Subcommittee had taken on
the U.H.F. problem, the only recommendations it made to the full
Commerce Committees were: 1. to establish an ad hoc advisory
committee to study further the whole field of allocations, 2. to
endorse the excise tax exemption on all-channel (including U.H.F.)
television receivers.[14] The most tangible result of the hearings
was that the networks, particularly N.B.C. and C.B.S., had become in
the minds of the public, and many Congressional leaders as well, the
villains who were causing the U.H.F. problem and any other problems
the industry might be experiencing. Therefore, as 1955 began, the
Senate Commerce Committee, under the prodding of Senator John W.
Bricker of Ohio, turned its attention to the television networks.

Investigations of "Network Monopoly"

The most serious official allegations that the networks might
be heavily to blame for the U.H.F. problem appeared in Special
Counsel Harry M. Plotkin's Senate Memorandum on Television Network
Regulation and the U.H.F. Problem released on February 1, 1955.[15]
In this Memorandum, Plotkin made a number of controversial sugges-
tions, including: 1. forcing networks to grant affiliation to
stations serving any area not yet served by a network affiliate,
2. restricting the amount of time any V.H.F. station in a market
with fewer than four V.H.F. outlets could devote to any one network's
programs, 3. selectively "de-intermixing" markets.[16]

On February 10th, a progress report by another Special Senate
Counsel, Robert F. Jones, concerning The Investigation of Television
Networks and the U.H.F.-V.H.F. Problem appeared.[17] Although milder
than the Plotkin Memorandum, Jones' report noted that the networks
had too much financial power over the industry. But Jones claimed
that there was too little information available to warrant Congressional action, and that U.H.F. might best be helped by some form of
voluntary action on the part of the networks.[18] The networks,
responding to both reports, but particularly to Plotkin's, termed
them the result of "antagonism by U.H.F. losers of affiliations"
against the networks.[19]

Armed with these two reports, Senator Bricker was able to nudge
the Senate Commerce Committee into a full scale television inquiry,
which although it lasted over two years and resulted in seven
published volumes of testimony,[20] resulted in no new legislation
concerning television.[21] This was despite Senator Bricker's introduction into both the 84th and 85th Congresses of strong network-
control bills, and issuing his own special report on Network
Monopoly in July of 1956.[22] This report market the highpoint of
Congressional criticism of the networks. Bricker claimed that the
data in it proved that:

> ... [the] networks ...have an unprecedented economic
> stranglehold on the Nation's television industry.
>   Effective competition is stifled under this yoke of
> economic dominance. The result is a private monopoly.[23]

Part of the reason why the Senate television hearings accomplished so little is that their effect was diluted by other

investigations which were going on simultaneously. In June of 1956

an Antitrust Subcommittee of the House Committee on the Judiciary

started hearings on "monopoly" in television,[24] and many in Congress

felt this subcommittee was the most appropriate one to make recom-

mendations concerning network power. Also, the F.C.C., seeing

Congressional displeasure with the Commission's position toward

network competition, had started its own "network study".[25] Since

the efforts of anti-network forces were diluted among the three

separate investigations, the networks were able to weather the storm.

No action was taken against them.

But while all these hearings into the evolving structure and

problems of the television industry were taking place, the F.C.C.

had already made a decision at the very start of the "post-freeze"

years which for all intents and purposes had decided the form which

the industry's structure would take. This fateful decision was the

approval of a merger between A.B.C. and United Paramount Theatres,

Inc. (U.P.T.).

The A.B.C.-U.P.T. Merger

During the "freeze", A.B.C., which like DuMont was having

serious financial problems with its television network, entered into

a merger agreement with U.P.T., which at the time was a financially

strong corporation. Since the merger would, from a legal stand-

point, involve the transfer of television stations to a different

owner, the newly formed American Broadcasting-Paramount Theatres,

Inc., F.C.C. approval was required. Hearings on the proposed merger began in January of 1952, and lasted until after the "freeze" had

been lifted, ending in August of 1952. The Commission's approval of

the merger came in a decision handed down on February 9, 1953.[26] The

F.C.C.'s stated reasons for approving the merger were that:

> A.B.C. has been unable to compete effectively
> with N.B.C. and C.B.S., principally because it lacks
> the financial resources, the working capital, and
> the diversity of revenue-producing activities
> [presumably this refers to equipment manufacturing]
> of the other networks or the companies with which
> they are associated. Increased financial resources
> are essential to enable A.B.C. to improve its
> program structure, build larger audiences, and
> thereby attract and retain sponsors and affiliates.[27]

This reasoning, while ignoring the role which the Commission's

own allocation plan had played in creating A.B.C.'s problems, was

to a large extent correct. What it left unmentioned was the probable

effect the merger would have on the ability of the other weaker

network, DuMont, in its struggle to compete. The then-president of

the DuMont network, Theodore Bergmann, stated in an interview many

years later that:

> ...when A.B.C., which was almost out of business,
> finally got its merger with United Paramount Theatres
> approved and received an infusion of capital to the tune
> of some thirty million dollars, the decision as to which
> network would be the third network, A.B.C. or DuMont,
> was made at that moment. The minute the F.C.C. approved
> that merger our [DuMont's] fate was sealed.[28]

Supporting this assessment of DuMont's competitive position

with respect to A.B.C. are the facts that in 1953, the year in which

the merger was approved, A.B.C. lost only $1.9 million compared to

DuMont's loss of $3.8 million, and in 1955, when DuMont gave up

national networking altogether, A.B.C. for the first time turned a

profit, earning $5.6 million from its television network opera-
tions.[29]

Despite the fact that the F.C.C. has never admitted that in
its approval of the merger it had consciously chosen to sacrifice
the DuMont network in order to save A.B.C., such a notion is not
all that far-fetched. As was mentioned before, the F.C.C.'s
primary concern in the oligopolistic competition it had always
envisioned for television broadcasting was that no one or two firms
(i.e. N.B.C. and C.B.S.) should dominate the industry as in radio.
But as the "freeze" ended, just such a situation had developed.
Since the station allocation plan in the Sixth Report and Order
was unable to support four national networks, but might be able to
support three, then if either A.B.C. or DuMont was to leave the
industry, the remaining third network might be able to develop
economic power equal to that of either N.B.C. or C.B.S. The only
question then, was who should leave and who should remain? True to
the behavior pattern predicted in Chapter I, the F.C.C., by approving
the A.B.C.-U.P.T. merger, in effect chose A.B.C. as the more likely
network to survive due to its radio broadcasting ties and experience,
and abandoned DuMont.

Although it is impossible to judge with certainty, if indeed
only one of the smaller two networks could have survived, then the
F.C.C.'s choice of A.B.C. as the third network with the better
chance of survival in competition with N.B.C. and C.B.S. most likely was
the correct one. However, the F.C.C.'s belief that a three-member

oligopoly with relatively equal-powered members would facilitate
performance in the public interest, was incorrect.

The Demise of DeMont

As mentioned in the previous section, the DuMont network had
lost $3.8 million in 1953, and by 1954 was frantically looking for a
way out of its predicament. After a plan to start a cable television
network was dropped due to the huge initial investment it would have
entailed, in October of 1954 a merger plan was worked out with
A.B.C.[30] A formal agreement was drawn up whereby A.B.C. would
absorb the DuMont network, picking up most of its affiliates and
putting the most popular DuMont shows in A.B.C.'s program lineup.
But the board of directors of Allen B. DuMont Laboratories, Inc.,
the network's parent company, turned down the proposed merger.[31]

With both sponsors and affiliates deserting what was clearly a
"sinking ship", on September 15, 1955 DuMont ceased its national
network operations. As the F.C.C. had hoped, DuMont's demise had a
salutary effect on A.B.C.'s fortunes. As can be seen in Table V-1,
although it would be several years before A.B.C. would be in a
position to challenge the frontrunning C.B.S. and N.B.C. networks,
in 1956 its advertising billings had already climbed to 16 percent
of the industry total. In addition, A.B.C.'s profits from television networking were just under $10 million, compared to the loss
of nearly $2 million it had incurred just three years earlier.[32]
A.B.C. was not on its way to becoming an equal partner in a network
triopoly that controlled an industry which had expanded greatly
since the end of the "freeze" in 1952.

Table V-1

Television Network Billings[a] 1953-1956

($ Millions)

	Total	N.B.C.	% of Total	C.B.S.	% of Total	A.B.C.	% of Total	DuMont	% of Total
1953	227.6	96.7	43%	97.5	43%	21.1	9%	12.4	5%
1954	320.2	126.1	39%	146.2	46%	34.7	11%	13.1	4%
1955	406.9	163.4	40%	189.0	46%	51.4	13%	3.1[b]	-[c]
1956	488.2	187.9	39%	223.5	46%	76.7	16%	-[b]	-[b]

[a] Network billings, which are not exact revenue figures due to discounts, etc., are nevertheless, accepted by the networks themselves, and by the industry generally, as a satisfactory index of comparison and trends.

[b] DuMont ceased national network operations on September 15, 1955.

[c] Less than one percent.

Note: Individual network's billings may not add up to industry total, nor their percents of the total to 100, due to rounding.

Source: Publishers' Information Bureau estimates appearing in Television Factbook, Number 27, Fall-Winter 1958, p. 27.

Industry Growth in the "Post-freeze" Years

During the period 1953-1956, the number of television stations
on the air had nearly quadrupled from the 122 at the end of 1952 to
459 at the end of 1956.[33] In addition, by the end of 1956, 71.8
percent of American homes had television, compared to a figure of
34.2 percent at the end of 1952.[34] Television had caught up with
and surpassed its predecessor, radio, during this period. In 1956
television broadcasting revenues were $896.9 million compared to
only $480.6 million for radio.[35] And as in previous periods, as the
television industry grew, concentration continued apace.

Concentration and Performance During the "Post-freeze" Years

During the period 1953-1956, when the television industry
attained the structure which persists to the present day, many of
the trends which had been noticed earlier, either continued or
levelled off at relatively peak values. Looking at Table V-2, it can
be seen that the essentially meaningless figure for network owned
stations as a share of total stations had fallen to 3.3 percent by
1956. In contrast, the figure for total affiliation, an overstate-
ment of network influence, hovered around 90 percent during the
entire period, with a value of 92.4 percent in 1956. The figures
for exclusive affiliation, after dropping off in 1953 from the 36.1
percent figure reached in 1952 (see Chapter IV, Table IV-2), due to
the large influx of stations, are particularly large by the end of
this period, reaching a height of 55.3 percent in 1956. This is due

Table V-2

Network Station Ownership and Affiliation 1953-1956

	Total Stations	Network Owned	% of Total	Network Affiliated	% of Total	Exclusive Affiliates	% of Total
1953	334	16	5.0%	310	92.8%	84	25.1%
1954	410	16	4.0%	365	89.0%	137	33.4%
1955	421	15	3.8%	379	90.0%	230	54.6%
1956	459	15	3.3%	424	92.4%	254	55.3%

Source: Compiled from the data on television stations' ownership and affiliation appearing in the Fall-Winter editions of Television Factbook in the years 1953-1956.

both to the further expansion of N.B.C. and C.B.S.'s influence, as well as to A.B.C.'s gaining a large number of exclusive affiliations after DuMont was out of the network picture. And although this exclusive affiliation figure may be the most reliable indicator of the trend in network concentration, it may still, as in earlier periods, understate the actual level of such concentration. One fact which tends to support such a notion is that in 1955, programs of the three national networks accounted for 78.2 percent of prime time programming on all (not just exclusive) affiliates.[36]

Looking now at Table V-3, it can be seen that the network share of industry revenues stayed near its earlier level of around 50 percent (see Chapter IV, Table IV-3), despite an actual decline in value from 53.5 percent in 1953 to 49.3 percent in 1956. That the networks were able to maintain such a high share of the industry's revenues is quite remarkable in light of the large number of new stations which entered the industry during this period. In addition, another important indicator of network concentration - profits, which also is presented in Table V-3, shows that the network share, which was 26.5 in 1953, jumped to over 40 percent in the succeeding years, with a value of 45.0 percent in 1956. Compared to the two previous indicators, the third one presented in Table V-3, the networks' share of industry assets, runs counter to the developing trend toward high levels of concentration. Whereas in 1952 the network asset share had reached a level of 54.7 percent (see Chapter IV, Table IV-3), by the end of 1953 the figure had plummeted to 28.7 percent of the industry total. By 1956 this figure had further

Table V-3

Television Industry Revenues, Profits, and Assets 1953-1956
($ Millions)

	Industry Revenues	Network Revenues	% of Industry	Industry Profits[a]	Network Profits[a]	% of Industry	Industry Assets[b]	Network Assets	% of Industry
1953	432.7	231.7	53.5%	68.0	18.0	26.5%	175.2	50.4	28.7%
1954	593.0	306.7	51.7%	90.3	36.5	40.4%	204.3	56.6	27.5%
1955	744.7	374.0	50.2%	150.2	68.0	45.3%	232.3	58.3	25.1%
1956	896.9	442.3	49.3%	189.6	85.4	45.0%	248.6	60.4	24.3%

[a] Before taxes.
[b] Depreciated value of tangible broadcast property.

Source: Federal Communications Commission, Final TV Broadcast Financial Data, 1953, 1954, 1955, 1956 (Washington, D.C., 1954, 1955, 1956, 1957).

declined to 24.3 percent. The explanation of this apparent anomaly is that most assets in the television industry are associated with the actual operation of stations (land, physical plant, equipment, etc.) and not with the operation of networks. Thus as the total number of stations in the industry increased rapidly, while the network owned stations remained constant (or declined slightly with DuMont's demise), it was to be expected that their share of total industry assets would decline. As a result, share of assets, like station ownership, is a poor indicator of the networks' concentration. Considering the fact that by 1956, the relevant concentration ratios presented in Tables V-2 and V-3 had reached levels of 40 and 50 percent, and that these were three firm ratios, it seems safe to conclude that television broadcasting had become a strong oligopoly industry. It now remains to be seen how the establishment of this strong oligopoly affected performance in the industry.

As was mentioned in Chapter IV, 1951 witnessed a dramatic improvement in the private performance of both the networks and the entire industry, although the latter's rate of return exceeded the former's by over 40 percent in 1952 (see Chapter IV, Table IV-4), and no clear trend had yet become visible. As can be seen in Table V-4, in 1953, with a large influx of unprofitable new stations into the industry, its rate of return fell from the value of 65.4 percent it had attained in 1952 (see Chapter IV, Table IV-4), to a low (relatively speaking) 38.8 percent in 1953. The network rate of return, however, climbed from its 1952 value of 21.3 percent (see Chapter IV, Table IV-4) to 35.7 percent in the first of the

Table V-4

Television Industry Rates of Return 1953-1956

	Industry Assets[a]	Industry Profits[b]	Rate of Return[c]	Network Assets[a]	Network Profits[b]	Rate of Return[c]
1953	175.2	68.0	38.8%	50.4	18.0	35.7%
1954	204.3	90.3	44.2%	56.6	36.5	64.5%
1955	232.3	150.2	64.7%	58.3	68.0	116.6%
1956	248.6	189.6	76.3%	60.4	85.4	141.4%

[a]Depreciated value of tangible broadcast property ($ Millions).
[b]Before taxes ($ Millions).
[c]Ratio of before-tax profits to depreciated value of tangible broadcast property.

Source: Federal Communications Commission, Final TV Broadcast Financial Data 1953, 1954, 1955, 1956 (Washington, D.C., 1954, 1955, 1956, 1957).

"post-freeze" years. In 1954, although the private performance of both the industry and the networks improved, the networks' did so dramatically, surpassing for the first time the figure for the entire industry. In 1955 and 1956, with DuMont gone and A.B.C. making profits, the rate of return for the networks jumped to values of 116.1 percent and 141.4 percent respectively, nearly doubling the industry's rate of return in those same years. Thus the consolidation of the network oligopoly into a strong triopoly, resulted in a fantastic improvement in their private performance, and to a lesser degree in an improvement in the industry's private performance as well.

Turning now to public performance, it can be seen in Table V-5, that data on program expenditures (the necessary but not sufficient factor in the quality of television programs) are only available for 1953. Nevertheless, for this year as previously, (see Chapter IV, Table IV-5) the networks outperform the industry, accounting for 69.0 percent of the total industry's expenditures on programming, and spending 64.3 percent of their total expenditures on programming compared to a figure of only 55.3 percent for the industry as a whole. In addition, testimony presented in two reports by the F.C.C.'s Office of Network Study tend to indicate that even after 1953, the networks consistently outspent the rest of the industry on programming.[37] It seems unlikely that this component of public performance was adversely affected by increasing network concentration during the "post-freeze" years.

Table V-5

Television Industry Program Expenditures 1953-1956

($ Millions)

	Industry Program Expenditures	Network Program Expenditures	Network % of Industry	Total Industry Expenditures	Total Network Expenditures	Industry Program % of Industry Total	Network Program % of Network Total
1953	199.2	137.4	69.0%	360.5	213.7	55.3%	64.3%
1954	n.a.	n.a.	n.a.	502.7	270.2	n.a.	n.a.
1955	n.a.	n.a.	n.a.	594.5	306.0	n.a.	n.a.
1956	n.a.	n.a.	n.a.	707.3	356.9	n.a.	n.a.

Note: n.a. - not available.

Source: Federal Communications Commission, Final TV Broadcast Financial Data 1953, 1954, 1955, 1956 (Washington, D.C., 1954, 1955, 1956, 1957).

Concerning the diversity component of public performance, it can be seen in Table V-6, that for network programming, Index #1, the indicator of quarter-hourly overall diversity, after reaching an all-time high value of 3.10 in 1953, had declined to a value of 2.00 in 1956. Similarly, Index #3, the indicator of daily overall diversity, shows a similar drop from an all time high value of 13.00 in 1953 to 9.29 in 1956. The indices for "specialized appeal" program diversity also fell. Index #2 fell from a value of 1.01 in 1953 to .62 in 1956, and Index #4 fell from 5.71 in 1953 to 3.00 in 1956. Calculating the percentage decline in Index #2 and Index #4 between 1953 and 1956, figures of 39 percent for the former and 47 percent for the latter result, both of which exceed the percentage decline in the number of networks which was only 25 percent.

A possible explanation of this phenomenon is that in 1953 with neither A.B.C. nor DuMont being able to afford "mass appeal" programs of the same quality (i.e. price) as N.B.C. and C.B.S., either, or both, of them may have chosen to appeal instead to the largest portion of the "specialized taste" television audience. The reasoning behind such a strategy would be that in this situation a large portion of the "specialized taste" audience might be larger than the small share of the "mass taste" audience which the weaker networks could hope to capture with their poorer quality programs. In 1956, however, with DuMont gone, and with increased resources available for programming, A.B.C. could now do battle with N.B.C. and C.B.S. for a share of the "mass taste" audience with the probability of gaining a larger audience than if it continued to appeal to a part (even the largest part) of the "specialized taste"

Table V-6

Television Program Diversity 1953–1956

Networks

	O.A.Q. Index #1	S.A.Q. Index #2	O.A.D. Index #3	S.A.D. Index #4
1953	3.10	1.01	13.00	5.71
1954	2.99	.85	11.71	4.57
1955	1.91	.69	9.71	3.71
1956	2.00	.62	9.29	3.00

Chicago

	O.A.Q. Index #1	S.A.Q. Index #2	O.A.D. Index #3	S.A.D. Index #4
1953	3.34	1.34	11.86	5.43
1954	3.33	1.18	13.00	5.71
1955	3.44	1.34	12.86	5.57
1956	3.46	1.30	12.86	5.14

New York

	O.A.Q. Index #1	S.A.Q. Index #2	O.A.D. Index #3	S.A.D. Index #4
1953	5.26	2.45	14.43	7.00
1954	4.79	1.83	14.29	6.00
1955	5.11	2.16	14.29	6.14
1956	4.95	2.11	14.43	6.14

Note: O.A.Q. - Overall quarter-hourly diversity indicator.
   S.A.Q. - "Specialized appeal" quarter-hourly
       diversity indicator.
   O.A.D. - Overall daily diversity indicator.
   S.A.D. - "Specialized appeal" daily diversity
       indicator.

Source: See Appendix.

audience. Thus the decline in the values of Index #2 and Index #4 may be the result of a combination of factors: one being DuMont's demise, and the other being the change in programming strategy on the part of A.B.C.

Looking now at the values of these indices for Chicago, which had four stations throughout this period, one of which became an independent, non-affiliated station after DuMont ceased operations, some contrasts with the network program situation appear. As expected, in 1956, the values of each of the indices, since Chicago had one more station offering programs than there were networks to do so, is higher than for network programming. But whereas the trends in the values of overall program diversity run counter to the network trends during this period, the values of Index #2 and Index #4, despite the lack of trends as in the network case, are nevertheless, lower in 1956 than in 1953.

Similarly, in looking at the diversity indices for New York programming, where seven stations operated throughout this period, one sees as one would expect, that the 1956 values of all indices are higher than for either the network or the Chicago program schedules. And although there are no trends in any of the four indices, as was the case with Chicago, the 1956 values of Index #2 and Index #4 are clearly lower than they were in 1953.

Thus, although station programming, particularly that of independent stations, may have acted to offset somewhat the decreases in overall network program diversity during the "post-freeze" years, these factors were less successful in offsetting the downward

trend in "specialized appeal" program diversity. Furthermore, the
offsetting effects on diversity which seem to flow from having more
stations in a market than there are national networks is not a widespread phenomenon, since only seven cities, in addition to New York
and Chicago, had more than three V.H.F. stations at this time, and
only one of these - Los Angeles, had more than four such stations.[38]

Except for several of the largest cities in the U.S. then, few
cities had enough stations to counteract the decreasing overall
program diversity reflected in the network program schedules in the
years 1953-1956. Furthermore it seems unlikely that any city's
station programming was able to counteract the even larger decrease
in "specialized appeal" program diversity which was reflected in
these network program schedules during this same period. Therefore
the welfare of a large number of viewers with "mass appeal" program
tastes, as well as the welfare of most, if not all, of those
viewers with "specialized appeal" program tastes, was adversely
affected by the downward trends in network program diversity which
occurred as the network oligopoly was consolidated into a powerful
triopoly in the years 1953-1956.

FOOTNOTES FOR CHAPTER V

[1] Television Factbook, Number 27, Fall-Winter 1958, p. 27.

[2] Sydney W. Head, Broadcasting in America Second Edition (Boston: Houghton Mifflin Co., 1972), p. 200.

[3] Ibid.

[4] Ibid.

[5] Federal Communications Commission, Final TV Broadcast Financial Data, 1953 (Washington, D.C., 1954), mimeo - no page numbers.

[6] Ibid.

[7] Ibid.

[8] Ibid.

[9] "Special Supplement on Allocations," Appendix A, Table 3, Television Digest, Volume XV, Number 19, April 27, 1959.

[10] Ibid.

[11] U.S. Senate, Committee on Interstate and Foreign Commerce, Subcommittee on Communications, 83rd Congress, 2nd Session, Hearings on Status of T.V. Stations and S. 3095 (Washington, D.C., 1954).

[12] Television Digest, Volume X, Number 21, May 22, 1954, pp. 4-5.

[13] Television Digest, Volume X, Number 25, June 19, 1954, pp. 4-5

[14] U.S. Senate, 83rd Congress, 2nd Session, Hearings on Status of T.V. Stations.

[15] U.S. Senate, Committee on Interstate and Foreign Commerce, 84th Congress, 1st Session, Television Network Regulation and the UHF Problem-Memorandum Prepared by Harry M. Plotkin, Special Counsel (Washington, D.C., 1955).

[16]Ibid, pp. 37-43.

[17]U.S. Senate, Committee on Interstate and Foreign Commerce, 84th Congress, 1st Session, Investigation of Television Networks and the UHF and VHF Problem - Progress Report Prepared by Robert F. Jones, Special Counsel (Washington, D.C., 1955).

[18]Ibid, pp. 5-8, 13-23.

[19]Television Digest, Volume XI, Number 7, February 12, 1955, pp. 4-5.

[20]U.S. Senate, Committee on Interstate and Foreign Commerce, 84th Congress, 2nd Session, and 85th Congress, 1st and 2nd Sessions, Television Inquiry (Washington, D.C., 1956, 1957, 1958). 7 volumes.

[21]Legislation passed much later in the 1960's and 1970's was based to some extent on information unearthed during this investigation.

[22]U.S. Senate, Committee on Interstate and Foreign Commerce, 84th Congress, 2nd Session, The Network Monopoly - Report Prepared by Senator John W. Bricker (Washington, D.C., 1956).

[23]Ibid, p. 1.

[24]U.S. House of Representatives, Committee on the Judiciary, Antitrust Subcommittee, 84th Congress, 2nd Session, Monopoly Problems in Regulated Industries - Part 2, Television (Washington, D.C., 1957). 4 volumes.

[25]The results of this study were published in U.S. House of Representatives, Committee on Interstate and Foreign Commerce, 85th Congress, 2nd Session, Network Broadcasting - Report of the Network Study Staff to the Network Study Committee of the Federal Communications Commission (Washington, D.C., 1957).

[26]U.S. House, 85th Congress, 2nd Session, Network Broadcasting, p. 80.

[27]Ibid.

[28]Theodore Bergmann, ex-president of the DuMont network, as quoted in Gary N. Hess, "An Historical Study of the DuMont Television Network," unpublished Ph.D. dissertation, Northwestern University, 1960, p. 140.

[29] U.S. House, 85th Congress, 2nd Session, Network Broadcasting, p. 576.

[30] Hess, "An Historical Study of DuMont," p. 114.

[31] Ibid, pp. 114-115.

[32] U.S. House, 85th Congress, 2nd Session, Network Broadcasting, p. 576.

[33] Television Factbook, Number 27, Fall-Winter 1958, p. 28.

[34] Ibid, p. 27.

[35] Ibid, p. 22.

[36] U.S. House, 85th Congress, 2nd Session, Network Broadcasting, pp. 192-193.

[37] U.S. House of Representatives, Committee on Interstate and Foreign Commerce, 88th Congress, 1st Session, Television Network Program Procurement, Second Interim Report by the Office of Network Study, Part I (Washington, D.C., 1963). Federal Communications Commission, Second Interim Report by the Office of Network Study - Television Network Program Procurement, Part II (Washington, D.C., 1965).

[38] U.S. House, 85th Congress, 2nd Session, Network Broadcasting, p. 27.

CHAPTER VI

CONCLUSIONS

This study has traced historically the development of the television network oligopoly. Given the institutional constraints of advertiser-support and government regulation, the economic theory was developed which would lead one to expect both the development of networks, and the divergence between private and public performance in television broadcasting.

It was shown that these institutional factors first arose in the radio broadcasting industry. They became part of that industry's legacy to television broadcasting, and fostered powerful radio networks which eventually extended their operations into television.

Although television experimentation was under way even as radio broadcasting began, the first commercial telecasts did not take place until 1941. This was the result both of the more complex technical problems involved in television, and of a reluctance on the part of the F.C.C. to allow premature television systems to be foisted on the public. Due to the intervention of World War II, the first commercial network broadcasting did not take place until 1948. But serious technical problems had arisen concerning television station allocation, and in September of 1948 the F.C.C. stopped processing new license applications, thus imposing a "freeze" upon the industry. At this time the television broadcasting industry was extremely small in comparison to its predecessor radio. Operations were unprofitable at both the station and network levels, and no trends were discernible in either private or public performance.

During the "freeze" years, 1949-1952, the complexion of the television industry changed. Despite the "freeze" lasting almost four years, many aspects of the industry expanded greatly. As Figure VI-I illustrates, network concentration was visible. N.B.C. and C.B.S., aided by the length and nature of the "freeze", had come to dominate television as they had radio before. During this period television broadcasting became profitable, although as can be seen in Figure VI-2, the networks' rate of return lagged behind that of the industry as a whole. Concerning public performance, although the networks outspent the industry on programming in this period, it can be seen Figures VI-3 and VI-4 that "specialized appeal" program diversity declined somewhat. Despite this, station programming in the Chicago and New York markets tended to reverse the networks' downward trend in "specialized appeal" programming in this period.

With the "freeze" lifted, the period 1953-1956 witnessed the industry developing the network structure it retains to the present day. The "uneconomic" station allocation plan which the F.C.C. had adopted when it lifted the "freeze" had led to a U.H.F. "problem" and charges of "network monopoly". Despite Congressional investigations of these charges, no action was taken concerning them. With the F.C.C.'s approval in 1953 of a merger between A.B.C. and United Paramount Theatres, Inc., the DuMont network's demise, and thus a network triopoly, was assured. Despite, or perhaps because of, the loss of one member, the networks' oliogopoly power increased in 1953-1956, as seen in Figure VI-I. The effect on private performance as the network concentration increased is seen in Figure VI-2.

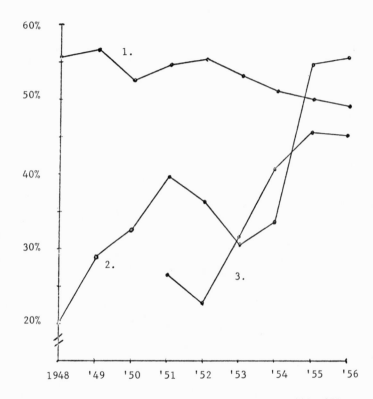

Figure VI-1: Television Network Concentration 1948-1956

Source: Drawn from data in Tables III-2, IV-2, IV-3, V-2, V-3.

Note: 1. Network Revenues as a % of industry revenues.
2. Exclusive network affiliates as a % of total stations.
3. Network profits as a % of industry profits.

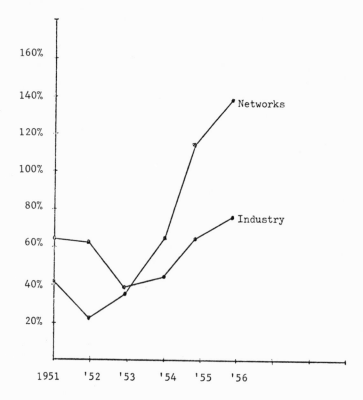

Figure VI-2: Television Industry and Networks' Rates
of Return 1951-1956[a]

[a]Neither the industry nor the networks
operated at a profit before 1951.

Source: Drawn from data in Tables IV-4,
V-4.

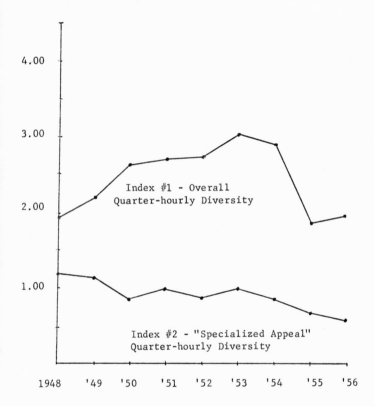

4.00

3.00

2.00

Index #1 - Overall
Quarter-hourly Diversity

1.00

Index #2 - "Specialized Appeal"
Quarter-hourly Diversity

1948   '49   '50   '51   '52   '53   '54   '55   '56

Figure VI-3:   Television Network Quarter-hourly
Diversity 1948-1956

Source: Drawn from data in Tables
III-3, IV-6, V-6.

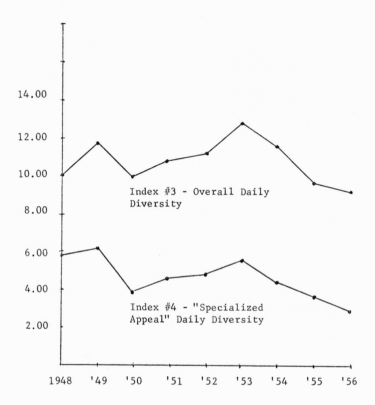

Figure VI-4: Television Network Daily Program
Diversity 1948-1956

Source: Same as Figure VI-3.

Network rates of return rise dramatically in this period, outstripping the industry as a whole. Public performance, although network program expenditures were not adversely affected, deteriorates in program diversity. As Tables VI-3 and VI-4 illustrate, "specialized appeal" program diversity has greatly declined, and even overall diversity goes down with the consolidation of the network oligopoly into a strong triopoly. In addition, station programming in the Chicago and New York markets was unable to offset completely the downward trend in "specialized appeal" program diversity which the network program schedules exhibited.

Unfortunately, the historical experience which has been recorded in this study does not lend itself to obvious policy recommendations concerning the television broadcasting industry. The long tradition of advertiser-support for commercial broadcasting and of government regulation, would caution against attempts either to "nationalize" the industry or abandon it to laissez-faire, on the grounds that performance, both private and public, might suffer from the massive disruption of the status quo. On the other hand, the same factors which contributed to the gap between public and private performance in the past, continue to operate today. There seems to be little chance that the situation is in any way self-correcting. Perhaps the only hope for improved public performance in television broadcasting lies outside the commercial sector in the field of "public" television. But even this is only a suggestion and is not meant to appear as a solution.

APPENDIX

TELEVISION PROGRAM DIVERSITY INDICES

The values of the four diversity indices which appear in this
study were obtained in the following manner. First, the weekly
program schedule for each station (or network) in the market under
consideration was coded according to the program types set out in
Table 1 for each quarter-hourly prime time (6-11 P.M.) period during
that week. Each individual index was then obtained as follows:
Index #1 - a quarter-hourly index of overall program diversity
calculated by summing the number of different program types broadcast
in each quarter hour prime time period during the week, and then
dividing this sum by one hundred and forty which is the number of
such time periods in a week. The values of this index could range
from one (perfect duplication) to n (perfect diversity), where n is
the number of stations (or networks) in the market.

Index #2 - a quarter-hourly index of "specialized appeal" program
diversity calculated by summing the number of different "specialized
appeal" program types broadcast in each quarter hour prime time
period during the week, and then dividing this sum by one hundred
and forty as was done in computing Index #1. The values of this
index could range from zero (no "specialized appeal" programming) to
n (all "specialized appeal" programming), where n is the number of
stations (or networks) in the market.

Index #3 - a daily index of overall program diversity calculated by summing the number of different program types broadcast on each day during the week, and then dividing this sum by seven which is the number of days in the week. The values of this index could range from one (perfect duplication) to twenty (perfect diversity), where twenty is the number of different program types.

Index #4 - a daily index of "specialized appeal" program diversity calculated by summing the number of different "specialized appeal" program types broadcast on each day during the week, and then dividing this sum by seven as was done in computing Index #3. The values of this index could range from zero (no "specialized appeal" programming) to eleven, where eleven is the number of different "specialized appeal" program types.

All weekly program schedules for New York and Chicago were obtained from the television listings for the first week in October (in order to get the new fall program lineups, but not have them distorted by special holiday programming which occurs in November and December) in the New York Times and Chicago Tribune respectively. Weekly program schedules for the national networks were obtained from the October issue of the magazine Television for the years 1948 to 1954, and from the October issue of the magazine Television Age for the years 1955 and 1956.

Table 1

Codes of Television Program Types

	Code	-	Description
	01	-	Mystery/Police/Lawyer
	02	-	Western
	03	-	Doctor/Hospital
	04	-	Adventure/Action
	05	-	Dramatic Series
	06	-	Comedy
"Mass Appeal"	07	-	Quiz/Game
Program	08	-	Variety/Light Music
Types	09	-	Sports

	10	-	News
	11	-	Feature Film
	12	-	Children's Program
	13	-	Educational/Instructional
	14	-	Documentary
	15	-	Serious Music
	16	-	Non-Series Drama
"Specialized	17	-	Religious
Appeal"	18	-	Foreign Language
Program	19	-	Talk/Interview/Editorial
Types	20	-	Cooking/Fashion/Travel/Other Popular Information

	99	-	No Scheduled Program

Source: The program codes were adapted from those appearing in Gary Steiner, The People Look at Television: A Study of Audience Attitudes (New York: Alfred A. Knopf, 1963); H. Land Associates, Television and the Wired City (Washington, D.C.: National Association of Broadcasters, 1968); Harvey J. Levin, "Program Duplication, Diversity, and Effective Viewer Choices: Some Empirical Findings," American Economic Review - Papers and Proceedings, Volume LXI, (May 1971).

BIBLIOGRAPHY

Government Documents

Federal Communications Commission, Annual Report. Washington, D.C.:
Government Printing Office, 1935-1957.

_____. Broadcast Financial Data for Networks and AM, FM and
Television Stations. Washington, D.C.: Government Printing
Office, 1946-1950.

_____. An Economic Study of Standard Broadcasting. Washington,
D.C.: Government Printing Office, 1947.

_____. Final TV Broadcast Financial Data. Washington, D.C.:
Government Printing Office, 1951-1957.

_____. Public Service Responsibility of Broadcast Licensees.
Washington, D.C.: Government Printing Office, 1946.

_____. Report on Chain Broadcasting. Washington, D.C.:
Government Printing Office, 1941.

_____. Second Interim Report by the Office of Network Study -
Television Network Program Procurement, Part II. Washington,
D.C.: Government Printing Office, 1965.

Federal Radio Commission. Annual Report. Washington, D.C.:
Government Printing Office, 1927-1934.

U.S. House of Representatives, Committee on the Judiciary, Antitrust
Subcommittee, 84th Congress, 2nd Session. Monopoly Problems in
Regulated Industries - Part 2, Television, Four Volumes.
Washington, D.C.: Government Printing Office, 1957.

_____, Committee on Interstate and Foreign Commerce, 85th
Congress, 2nd Session. Network Broadcasting - Report of the
Network Study Staff to the Network Study Committee of the
Federal Communications Commission. Washington, D.C.: Govern-
ment Printing Office, 1957.

_____, _____, 88th Congress, 1st Session, Television
Network Program Procurement, Second Interim Report by the
Office of Network Study of the Federal Communications Commission,
Part I. Washington, D.C.: Government Printing Office, 1963.

Economic Report of the President, 1973. Washington, D.C.: Government
Printing Office, 1973.

U.S. President's Task Force on Communications Policy. <u>Staff Paper Six - Part I</u>. Washington, D.C.: Government Printing Office, 1969.

U.S. Senate, Committee on Interstate and Foreign Commerce, 85th Congress, 2nd Session. <u>Allocation of T.V. Channels - Report of the Ad Hoc Advisory Commitee on Allocations</u>. Washington, D.C.: Government Printing Office, 1958.

_____, _____, Subcommittee on Communications, 83rd Congress, 2nd Session. <u>Hearings on Status of T.V. Stations and S. 3095</u>. Washington, D.C.: Government Printing Office, 1954.

_____, _____, 84th Congress, 1st Session. <u>Investigation of Television Networks and the UHF and VHF Problem - Progress Report Prepared by Robert F. Jones, Special Counsel</u>. Washington, D.C.: Government Printing Office, 1955.

_____, _____, 84th Congress, 2nd Session. <u>The Network Monopoly - Report Prepared by Senator John W. Bricker</u>. Washington, D.C.: Government Printing Office, 1956.

_____, _____, 84th Congress, 2nd Session, and 85th Congress, 1st and 2nd Sessions. <u>Television Inquiry, Seven Volumes</u>. Washington, D.C.: Government Printing Office, 1956-1958.

_____, _____, 84th Congress, 1st Session. <u>Television Network Regulation and the UHF Problem - Memorandum Prepared by Harry M. Plotkin, Special Counsel</u>. Washington, D.C.: Government Printing Office, 1955.

<u>Personal Interviews</u>

Interview with Allen B. DuMont, Jr., son of the late founder of the Dumont television network, August 14, 1972.

<u>Newspapers and Trade Journals</u>

<u>The Chicago Tribune</u>. 1946-1957.

<u>The New York Times</u>. 1946-1957.

<u>Television</u>. Manchester, N.H.: Frederick Kugel Co., Inc. Volumes I - XIV. 1944-1957.

<u>Television Age</u>, New York: Television Editorial Corporation. Volumes
I - V. 1953-1957.

<u>Television Digest</u>. Radnor Penn.: Triangle Publications, Inc.,
Volumes I - XIII. 1945-1957.

<u>Television Factbook</u>. Radnor, Penn.: Triangle Publications, Inc.,
Numbers 1 - 27. 1945-1958.

<u>Radio Annual and Television Yearbook</u>. New York: Radio Daily Corpora-
tion. 1946-1957.

Books

Archer, Gleason L. <u>Big Business and Radio</u>. New York: The American
Historical Society, Inc., 1939.

Archer, Gleason L. <u>History of Radio to 1926</u>. New York: The American
Historical Society, Inc., 1938.

Banning, William P. <u>Commercial Broadcasting Pioneer: the WEAF Experiment 1922-1926</u>. Cambridge, Mass.: Harvard University Press,
1946.

Barnouw, Erik. <u>A History of Broadcasting in the United States, Three
Volumes</u>. New York: Oxford University Press, 1966.

Chester, Giraud and Garnet R. Garrison and Edgar E. Willis. <u>Tele-
vision and Radio</u>. New York: Appleton-Century-Crofts, 1963.

Danielian, N.R. <u>A.T.&T., The Story of Industrial Conquest</u>. New
York: The Vanguard Press, 1939.

Emery, Walter B. <u>Broadcasting and Government</u>. East Lansing,
Michigan State University Press, 1968.

Harlow, Alvin F. <u>Old Wires and New Waves</u>. New York: D. Appleton-
Century Co., 1936.

Head, Sydney W. <u>Broadcasting in America</u>. Boston: Houghton Mifflin
Co., 1956.

Head, Sydney W. <u>Broadcasting in America, Second Edition</u>. Boston:
Houghton Mifflin Co., 1972.

Hubbell, Richard. <u>4000 Years of Television</u>. New York: Putnam and
Sons, Inc., 1942.

Kaysen, Carl and Donald F. Turner. Antitrust Policy, An Economic and Legal Analysis. Cambridge, Mass.: Harvard University Press, 1959.

Kohlmeier, Louis M. The Regulators. New York: Harper and Row, Inc., 1969.

Land, H.W., Associates. Television and the Wired City. Washington, D.C., National Association of Broadcasters, 1968.

Lee, Robert E. Television. New York: Essential Books, Inc., 1944.

Levin, Harvey J. The Invisible Resource. Baltimore: The Johns Hopkins Press, 1971.

MacLaurin, W. Rupert. Invention and Innovation in the Radio Industry. New York: The Macmillan Co., 1949.

Robinson, Thomas Porter. Radio Networks and the Federal Government. New York: Columbia University Press, 1943.

Schiller, Herbert I. Mass Communications and American Empire. New York: Augustus M. Kelley, Inc., 1969.

Siepman, Charles A. Radio's Second Chance. Boston: Little, Brown and Co., 1946.

Steinger, Gary. The People Look at Television: A Study of Audience Attitudes. New York: Alfred A. Knopf, 1963.

Waldrop, Frank C. and Joseph Barkin. Television, a Struggle for Power. New York: William Morrow Co., 1938.

Articles

Benson, S.M. and R. Soligo. "The Economics of the Network-Affiliate Relationship in the Television Broadcasting Industry," American Economic Review, Volume LXIII, (June 1973).

Coase, R.H. "The Federal Communications Commission," Journal of Law and Economics, Volume II, (October 1959).

Crandall, Robert W. "The Economic Effect of Television-Network Program 'Ownership'," Journal of Law and Economics, Volume XIV, (October 1971).

Goldin, H.H. "Economic and Regulatory Problems in the Broadcasting Field," Land Economics, Volume XXX, (August 1954).

Greenberg, Edward and Harold J. Barnett. "TV Program Diversity -
New Evidence and Old Theories," American Economic Review -
Papers and Proceedings, Volume LXI, (May 1971).

Levin, Harvey J. "Economic Effects of Broadcast Licensing,"
Journal of Political Economy, Volume LXXII, (April 1964).

_____. "Federal Control of Entry in the Broadcasting Industry,"
Journal of Law and Economics, Volume V, (October 1962).

_____. "Program Duplication, Diversity, and Effective Viewer
Choices: Some Empirical Findings," American Economic Review -
Papers and Proceedings, Volume LXI, (May 1971).

_____. "Spectrum Allocation Without Market," American Economic
Review - Papers and Proceedings, Volume LX, (May 1970).

McGowan, John J. "Competition, Regulation, and Performance in
Television Broadcasting," Washington University Law Quarterly,
Volume 1967, (Fall 1967).

Steiner, Peter O. "Program Patterns and Preferences and the
Workability of Competition in Radio Broadcasting," Quarterly
Journal of Economics, LXVI, (May 1952).

Other Sources

Eoyang, Thomas T. "An Economic Study of the Radio Industry in the
United States of America," unpublished Ph.D. dissertation,
Columbia University, 1936.

Hess, Gary N. "An Historical Study of the DuMont Television
Network," unpublished Ph.D. dissertation, Northwestern
University, 1960.

Kittross, John M. "Television Frequency Allocation Policy in the
United States," unpublished Ph.D. dissertation, University of
Illinois, 1959.

VITA

Stewart Louis Long was born on October 28, 1943, in Cornwall, New York. He received a B.A. degree in economics from Hunter College of the City University of New York in 1970. He received a M.A. degree in economics from the University of Illinois in 1972, and was elected to Omicron Delta Epsilon.

While attending the University of Illinois he was a National Science Foundation Trainee for the period 1970-1973. He received a Lilly Foundation grant for dissertation research in the Fall of 1972, and an Earhart Foundation fellowship for dissertation research in the Summer of 1973. During the academic year 1972-1973 he was a teaching assistant in the Department of Economics at the University of Illinois, and he received the Robert E. Demarest Memorial Award for outstanding teaching by a graduate student for the Fall semester 1972.

He was appointed an Assistant Professor of Economics at California State University, Fullerton, for the academic year 1973-1974.

DISSERTATIONS IN BROADCASTING

An Arno Press Collection

Bailey, Robert Lee. **An Examination of Prime Time Network Television Special Programs, 1948 to 1966.** *(Doctoral Thesis, University of Wisconsin, 1967)* **1979**

Burke, John Edward. **An Historical-Analytical Study of the Legislative and Political Origins of the Public Broadcasting Act of 1967.** *(Doctoral Dissertation, The Ohio State University, 1971)* **1979**

Foley, K. Sue. **The Political Blacklist in the Broadcast Industry:** The Decade of the 1950s. *(Doctoral Dissertation, The Ohio State University, 1972)* **1979**

Hess, Gary Newton. **An Historical Study of the Du Mont Television Network.** *(Doctoral Dissertation, Northwestern University, 1960)* **1979**

Howard, Herbert H. **Multiple Ownership in Television Broadcasting:** Historical Development and Selected Case Studies. *(Doctoral Dissertation, Ohio University, 1973)* **1979**

Jameson, Kay Charles. **The Influence of the United States Court of Appeals for the District of Columbia on Federal Policy in Broadcast Regulation, 1929-1971.** *(Doctoral Dissertation, University of Southern California, 1972)* **1979**

Kirkley, Donald Howe, Jr. **A Descriptive Study of the Network Television Western During the Seasons 1955-56 to 1962-63.** *(Doctoral Dissertation, Ohio University, 1967)* **1979**

Kittross, John Michael. **Television Frequency Allocation Policy in the United States.** *(Doctoral Dissertation, University of Illinois, 1960)* **1979**

Larka, Robert. **Television's Private Eye:** An Examination of Twenty Years Programming of a Particular Genre, 1949 to 1969. *(Doctoral Dissertation, Ohio University, 1973)* **1979**

Long, Stewart Louis. **The Development of the Television Network Oligopoly.** *(Doctoral Thesis, University of Illinois at Urbana-Champaign, 1974)* **1979**

MacFarland, David T. **The Development of the Top 40 Radio Format.** *(Doctoral Thesis, University of Wisconsin, 1972)* **1979**

McMahon, Robert Sears. **Federal Regulation of the Radio and Television Broadcast Industry in the United States, 1927-1959:** With Special Reference to the Establishment and Operation of Workable Administrative Standards. *(Doctoral Dissertation, The Ohio State University, 1959)* **1979**

Muth, Thomas A. **State Interest in Cable Communications.** *(Doctoral Dissertation, The Ohio State University, 1973)* 1979

Pearce, Alan. **NBC News Division:** A Study of the Costs, the Revenues, and the Benefits of Broadcast News and **The Economics of Prime Time Access.** *(Doctoral Dissertation, Indiana University, 1972)* 1979

Pepper, Robert M. **The Formation of the Public Broadcasting Service.** *(Doctoral Dissertation, University of Wisconsin, 1975)* 1979

Pirsein, Robert William. **The Voice of America:** A History of the International Broadcasting Activities of the United States Government, 1940-1962. *(Doctoral Dissertation, Northwestern University, 1970)* 1979

Ripley, Joseph Marion, Jr. **The Practices and Policies Regarding Broadcasts of Opinions about Controversial Issues by Radio and Television Stations in the United States.** *(Doctoral Dissertation, The Ohio State University, 1961)* 1979

Robinson, Thomas Porter. **Radio Networks and the Federal Government.** 1943

Sadowski, Robert Paul. **An Analysis of Statutory Laws Governing Commercial and Educational Broadcasting in the Fifty States.** *(Doctoral Thesis, The University of Iowa, 1973)* 1979

Schwarzlose, Richard Allen. **The American Wire Services:** A Study of Their Development as a Social Institution. *(Doctoral Thesis, University of Illinois at Urbana-Champaign, 1965)* 1979

Smith, Ralph Lewis. **A Study of the Professional Criticism of Broadcasting in the United States. 1920-1955.** *(Doctoral Thesis, University of Wisconsin, 1959)* 1979

Stamps, Charles Henry. **The Concept of the Mass Audience in American Broadcasting:** An Historical-Descriptive Study. *(Doctoral Dissertation, Northwestern University, 1956)* 1979

Steiner, Peter O. **Workable Competition in the Radio Broadcasting Industry.** *(Doctoral Thesis, Harvard University, 1949)* 1979

Stern, Robert H. **The Federal Communications Commission and Television:** The Regulatory Process in an Environment of Rapid Technical Innovation. *(Doctoral Thesis, Harvard University, 1950)* 1979

Tomlinson, John D. **International Control of Radiocommunications.** 1945

Ulloth, Dana Royal. **The Supreme Court:** A Judicial Review of the Federal Communications Commission. *(Doctoral Dissertation, University of Missouri-Columbia, 1971)* 1979